HOW TO MAKE COLLEGES WANT YOU

Insider Secrets for Tipping the Admissions Odds in Your Favor

MIKE MOYER

Foreword by Michael Behnke,
Vice President and Dean of Enrollment,
The University of Chicago

SOURCEBOOKS, INC.
NAPERVILLE, ILLINOIS

This publication is designed to provide accurate and authoritative information in regard to the subject matter covered. It is sold with the understanding that the publisher is not engaged in rendering legal, accounting, or other professional service. If legal advice or other expert assistance is required, the services of a competent professional person should be sought.—*From a Declaration of Principles Jointly Adopted by a Committee of the American Bar Association and a Committee of Publishers and Associations*

All brand names and product names used in this book are trademarks, registered trademarks, or trade names of their respective holders. Sourcebooks, Inc., is not associated with any product or vendor in this book.

Published by Sourcebooks, Inc.
P.O. Box 4410, Naperville, Illinois 60567-4410
(630) 961-3900
Fax: (630) 961-2168
www.sourcebooks.com

Library of Congress Cataloging-in-Publication Data

Moyer, Mike.

  How to make colleges want you : insider secrets for tipping the admissions odds in your favor / Mike Moyer.

     p. cm.

  Includes bibliographical references and index.

  1. Universities and colleges--United States--Admission--Handbooks, manuals, etc. 2. Universities and colleges--United States--Admission. I. Title.

  LB2351.2.M69 2008

  378.1'610973--dc22

2008015086

Printed and bound in the United States of America.

CHG 10 9 8 7 6 5 4 3 2 1

This book is dedicated to Anson and Merrily—
I hope it helps them in 2023.

CONTENTS

FOREWORD

The director of my community choral group sometimes runs out of concrete suggestions for how to learn or shape a musical passage. Then he resorts to telling us, "Just sing better!" In this book, Mike Moyer actually offers many concrete suggestions on how to improve your chances of admission to a great college. But they can all be summarized in a phrase as general as "Sing better." The phrase is: "Be more interesting!"

Admissions deans are usually not overly fond of books like this. We are always looking for students who are "genuine"—students who excel in class because they love learning and are curious, or students who are championship debaters because they love to debate. Students who get good grades or win debate tournaments only because it will look good on a transcript often come across as packaged and uninteresting. Books like this can be seen as helping the latter kind of student look more like the former.

In this book, however, Mike Moyer urges the long view, not the short-term tricks approach, and he gives valuable and novel ideas on how young people can "be more interesting." You have to start somewhere on the road to a more fulfilling life. Robert Frost was not born a great poet. As he said, "You are always believing ahead of your evidence. What was the evidence that I could write a poem? I just believed it."

The college search process can be stressful and unrewarding. But many students find that it can be a valuable time for self-reflection. What do you like about yourself? What do you like about your peers? Do your friends reinforce or undermine the characteristics about yourself that you like and want to develop? "Being more interesting" can mean risking alienation from some peers who value conformity. Are you ready to risk that?

Raising homing pigeons is a rather weird thing to do. (Read the book to understand the reference.) The author risked ridicule when he did that. But maybe the ridicule was from conformist people whose opinions shouldn't have counted for much. The singer/composer Beatle Paul McCartney, in one of his less eloquent but insightful moments, said, "I used to think that anyone doing anything weird was weird. I suddenly realized that anyone doing anything weird wasn't weird at all and that it was the people saying they were weird that were weird."

This book encourages you to be a little bit weird and to develop things that distinguish you from others. Doing that cannot help but make you a more interesting and fulfilled person. And admissions officers are likely to notice.

I have a closing suggestion for how to distinguish yourself not only from other teenagers, but also from most everybody else: read good books, including this one.

MICHAEL BEHNKE
VICE PRESIDENT AND DEAN OF COLLEGE ENROLLMENT
THE UNIVERSITY OF CHICAGO
FALL 2007

INTRODUCTION

I n the spring of 1990, I graduated from my high school, Thayer Academy, in Braintree, Massachusetts. The then Chief Justice of the United States, William Rehnquist, was the keynote speaker. His appearance was a very big deal, shrouded in secrecy and security. I can't remember a word he said. I was way too busy thinking about how excited I was to be going to college in the fall.

Thayer Academy was, and still is, a well-regarded college prep school on the south shore of Boston. The reputation is good, the teachers are good, and the facilities are good. I remember being especially impressed with the new multi-million-dollar science building, complete with a state-of-the-art set of weather instruments in the lobby and a huge mainframe computer with spinning discs, not unlike those in the background of Dr. Evil's underground lair from *Austin Powers*. I had dreams of becoming a doctor or a veterinarian and fancied myself as a science whiz. There was one problem—I wasn't a science whiz. In fact, I wasn't a whiz at anything.

I was shy and covered with zits. I wasn't very good at sports, I didn't do very many extracurricular activities, and I didn't have a steady job. I had kissed *one* girl *one* time.[1] My SAT scores were okay at 1140, but my grades were terrible; I graduated with a 2.04 weighted GPA.

---

1. It was on my graduation day. She kissed *everyone* that day.

All my life I had terrible grades. I can remember constantly being told that I was a "smart kid who didn't apply himself." My teachers always took me aside to tell me to "get serious" about my schoolwork, and to "stop sleeping" in class. My parents warned me time and time again that doors would be slammed in my face if I didn't improve my grades. I could tell they were frustrated, and so was I. I felt like I *was* working as hard as I possibly could.

During my senior year in high school I applied to colleges, just like everyone else. My guidance counselor gave me a long list of schools because she feared the chances that I would be accepted at any of them were slim. I picked the most competitive colleges on the list because I was delusional. (Remember, I thought I was a science whiz. Even after my biology teacher refused to write me a recommendation, I *still* thought I was a science whiz.)

However, when I applied to a lot of competitive colleges, I got accepted to *all* of them. The headmaster, teachers, and coaches were openly amazed. Nobody could figure out how I got in; were the colleges blind?

It happened again five years later. With a mere 2.6 college GPA, I applied to two highly competitive graduate schools. I didn't have many good relationships with professors, so I had to ask a virtual *stranger* to write my recommendation. I was accepted to both schools. My friends were in shock. I knew other students with a much better academic record who got rejected from less competitive graduate programs.

I went to Northwestern for a master's degree, and I did quite well. Several years later I was accepted to business school at the University of Chicago; it was recently ranked number one.[2]

---

2. Rankings don't matter (unless you're number one).

I am the cofounder of Cappex.com, a company that helps kids find the right college, and I'm also the founder of College Peas (www. CollegePeas.com), a company that helps kids learn how to get into college. I live and breathe college admissions, and I've spoken to hundreds of high school counselors, college admissions deans, and college admissions counselors. They are the Gatekeepers, and they hold all the keys. They will let the right kids through, and quite often the right kids don't even know they're the right kids (like me). The people who work in admissions all have a common characteristic—they value education, and they want to share it with the world. They are on your side.

I have spent countless hours with admissions professionals learning about the admissions process and what they look for in prospective students. Their messages are consistent. Most people think colleges seek "high-quality students," and to most people this means good grades, high test scores, a laundry list of extracurricular activities, recommendations written by important people, and clever essays written with just the right mix of humor and profound insight. While this is technically true, and these things are nice, at the end of the day colleges will opt for diversity and authenticity. That means that as long as you can convince them that you can handle the work, they will move past the typical application elements in favor of someone who brings a new perspective to their campus and someone who shows a real passion.

It is now clear to me why I fared so well in the admissions game. To the world, I was a mild-mannered teenager. To the admissions counselor, I was a superhero. My willingness to travel far from home helped provide important geographic diversity. My selection of and commitment to a quirky hobby positioned me as a man with passion and sensitivity. The people I engaged in the process helped convince the colleges that I could keep up with the work even though my past performance said otherwise.

This book is an explanation of the actions I took that enabled me to win the admissions game against the odds, and you can apply these tips to your college search. The things I did made my GPA and test scores much less important to the admissions department. Today, with the benefit of hindsight, research, and experience, I can now share these ideas with you so that you, too, can get the edge you will need regardless of your academic record. The things I did enabled me to successfully compete against other students who had much more solid academic credentials and much more active extracurricular schedules.

When I applied to college, I did these things by *accident*. I had no idea I was doing things that gave me a serious edge over other applicants. You can do these things on purpose and achieve even greater results than I did.

Common wisdom tells us that in order to succeed, you must work harder and do better than the competition. All my life, people told me to work harder or be more organized or develop better study habits. This just isn't so. It's more important to be different, and lucky for you, being different doesn't necessarily require you to work harder or do better than the competition.

In admissions, too much attention is focused on the details of the application itself. Former Chief Justice of the United States William Rehnquist once said, "I used to worry about every little footnote… Now I realize you just need five votes."

Such is the way of college admissions. It's not about how well-written your essay is or how good your grades are. Don't get me wrong—grades and good essays are really important. (They are especially important if that's all you have to offer.) But what you really need are a few people who believe in you[3] and who are willing to cast their vote in your favor. Do that and you have it made. Those people are out there. They are looking for you, and they *do* want to help you. You just have to make sure they find you.

---

3. It may sound corny, but it's true!

Chapter 1

UNDERSTANDING ADMISSIONS

U p until now, there have been few events in your life that have been as significant as your passage from high school to college. The fact that you even made the decision to pursue a college career is a big step in the right direction. Most people in this world lack the opportunity, let alone the choice, to pursue a college education. And if you are serious about your decision to go to college, you *will* go to college, it *will* be great, you *will* be able to pay for it, and you *will* reap the benefits of a college education.

Virtually all people who really want to go to college *can* go to college. There are no real barriers. Many people think they can't afford college. They look at the fat tuition price tag and freak out. Don't worry—fat price tags are misleading. If you need money for college, it is available. In fact, the more you need, the more you will probably get, and often, the more will be in the form of scholarships and grants that you won't have to pay off. But even if you can afford it, many people feel like colleges are just too hard to get into. The truth is that most colleges aren't very hard to get into. In fact, the vast majority of colleges, even famous and big-name colleges, aren't very competitive at all.

In spite of the fact that most colleges are fairly easy to get into, many people feel a sense of accomplishment when they get accepted to a college that doesn't take "just anybody." Getting accepted to a competitive college feels good. It makes you feel like all your work up to now has been worth it. If that is you, then I say, "Go for it." Setting a standard and goals for yourself is a fine idea. But there is a more important reason that positioning yourself to be accepted at a competitive college is important.

Fit

People worry so much about how they are going to get into college that few of them put much thought into how they are going to get out of college. When it comes to getting into college, your chances are quite high. However, when it comes to getting out, it's a different story. Many students who start college never finish at the place they started, and many never finish at all. According to the National Center for Education Statistics, 23 percent of students entering college will wind up transferring, and only 54 percent of students will actually graduate within *six* years. We put a lot of emphasis on getting in, but the real issue isn't getting in, it's finding the right fit.

When it comes to getting the most out of college, fit is everything. Fit will determine your happiness, your success, and even whether you will graduate. A bad fit is a bad thing. Finding the right fit, however, can be tricky. Because of this, it's important to have choices. The more choices you have, the better your chances of finding the right fit. The best students, those who are real contenders for highly competitive colleges like Harvard, Stanford, Northwestern, and University of Chicago, have lots of choices. They can pretty much pick any school they want. And, as a result, many of them pick a college that is a good fit. Granted, these kids are good students anyway, but don't underestimate fit. I personally know many top students who transferred out of their original choice or dropped out completely. Students who get admitted to competitive colleges tend to graduate at much higher rates than other students.

So, the moral of the story is that the more choices you have, the better your chances of finding the right fit. And, if you can make yourself a contender for competitive colleges, the number of choices you have will grow substantially.

When I applied to colleges, I wanted to get accepted to a competitive college. I had the odds stacked against me because I was a terrible student, but I had to prove to myself that I could get into a place that didn't take everybody. Based on my academic record, I shouldn't have been accepted at any competitive colleges. Some might argue that my academic record made me a questionable choice for even non-competitive colleges. But somehow I stumbled upon the techniques in this book and wound up getting accepted to competitive colleges.

Despite getting accepted at competitive colleges, I decided to attend the University of Kansas (KU). (At the time, University of Kansas was not very competitive.) I chose KU because when I went to visit, it felt like the right place for me. All the competitive colleges

I visited just didn't seem like a place where I'd be happy. KU was great. I went to lots of parties, made lots of friends, and learned lots of things (both inside and outside of class). I changed so much after a couple of years at KU that my prep-school friends no longer recognized me. I was a changed man, and I have never regretted rejecting the colleges to which I had so dearly wanted to be accepted. KU was the right fit for me, and you should search for the right fit for you, regardless of how "competitive" the college may be.

Colleges Want You

Popular media would have you believe that colleges are awash with quality applications and are becoming more competitive than ever. The hype tells you that colleges can have their pick of the litter when it comes to students and unless you're a hotshot with a resume a mile long, you will never get in. There are thousands of colleges that can provide an extremely solid education. They want you; they are looking for you every day. Colleges actively reach out to students and try to entice them to attend. They spend millions of dollars on marketing and hire armies of people to figure out who and where you are. They set up huge scholarship funds to help you pay your way. They hold networking events across the country in an attempt to stimulate referrals. Colleges are after you this very minute. Colleges don't go through this effort just to reject you. They want you to show up ready to learn and ready to participate in all they have to offer.

The colleges that are actively looking for you aren't bottom-feeders. They are great colleges. Even Stanford has admissions counselors who are combing the globe for the right students.

Competitive colleges, especially highly competitive colleges, are among the most aggressive marketers. In fact, that's a big part of what makes them competitive. It's not just the quality of education that makes them competitive; it's also the quality of their marketing efforts. Better marketing leads to more applications, which leads to competitive admissions. Rest assured, they want you—they really want you! In fact, it's quite strange that so much of college admissions has been built up to seem like a big test. It's as if getting into college is some kind of rite of passage. It isn't. *Going* to college may be, but getting in doesn't have to be.

As you get closer and closer to applying to college, it gets harder and harder to change your academic and extracurricular record. When you're a senior, you can't say, "Oops! I need to play a freshman sport!" It is for this reason that people freak out so much about essays, recommendations, and the dreaded standardized tests. With application due dates crashing down upon them, they begin to fear that they didn't do all they could do to be good college candidates. You may think that essays, recommendations, and standardized tests can make or break you in the college admissions process. If you think this, then you are reading the right book, because while essays, recommendations, and standardized tests are important, there are much more important things you can do to make the difference.

If you are one of the hundreds of thousands of students hankering for a shot at a competitive college, you are reading the right book. The ideas in this book will *dramatically* increase your chances of getting into the college of your choice, just like they did for me. No matter where you are in your high school career,

if you start these things today, the chance you will get into the competitive college of your choice will improve.

The ideas in this book are pretty straightforward and none of them are really that hard to implement. However, this is not a book of tricks. The ideas are designed to actually transform you into the type of applicant colleges are out there trying to find. Colleges need more unique students who will add diversity and flair to their campuses.

The concepts in this book are based on my research and experience as the cofounder of Cappex.com and the founder of College Peas, as well as my real-life experience as a terrible student who managed to stand out and get accepted to many competitive colleges. If I were the average kid, I would have been thrown to the wolves in college admissions, but I stumbled upon a few things that made the difference. The good news is that my mistakes can become your strategy. Even if you just squeaked by in high school, the ideas I'll show you will give you a second chance at a competitive college. Not all colleges are competitive, so you really don't have to worry that much about getting in, but if you want to get into a competitive college, I can show you how.

The Seventy-Seventy Rule

The admissions industry throws around the seventy-seventy phrase, which means that 70 percent of colleges accept more than 70 percent of their applicants. This means there are thousands of colleges that accept *more* than 70 percent of the students who apply. In some cases these colleges accept virtually every applicant. Just because a college doesn't reject lots of students doesn't mean it's a bad college. Some colleges, like many state colleges for example, admit any student who has a GED or a high school diploma from within the state.

Getting into a non-competitive college is easy. Simply find their application online, fill it out, click "submit," and tell everyone that you were accepted to college and you're going to spend the summer hanging out in front of a convenience store.[4] I'm serious—applying to a non-competitive college is a real choice that you face right now. If you decide to take it, you can return this book to the person you borrowed it from. If you decide, however, to press forward and apply to a competitive college, read on (and buy your own copy!).

Competitive Colleges

A competitive college is one that actually reviews at least some (if not all) of the applications it receives and makes a judgment call as to whether the applicant will be a good fit with their community. When most people think about competitive colleges, they are thinking Ivy League, or they are thinking about those that typically make the *U.S. News & World Report* top-ten list, such as Harvard, Stanford, Yale, Northwestern, University of Chicago, Princeton, or Dartmouth. These are *highly* competitive colleges, and many of the students who are admitted to these colleges got there at the expense of their childhood and (in some cases) their sanity. Few, if any, are geniuses.[5] If you're a serious contender for any of these colleges, you probably have a swarm of teachers,

---

4. You might want to consider a summer job. You'll need money for books and, if you are twenty-one, beer.

5. More on this later, but remember: people who make good grades aren't necessarily smart, and smart people don't necessarily make good grades.

coaches, and guidance counselors advising you already, and you may not need my help.

For the purposes of this book, however, we are going to refer to a competitive college as one that rejects more than 35 percent of its applicants. This covers roughly 25 percent of the colleges in the United States, including all the Ivy League colleges and most of the colleges you'll find listed in *U.S. News* rankings. It also includes most of the colleges people think of as "good" colleges, plus a lot of really nice private liberal arts colleges or smaller state colleges you probably haven't even heard of.[6] You can be proud to go to any of these colleges. They are all excellent and many of them are looking for students like you right now.

I've found that competitive colleges like to attract students with GPAs over 3.0, SAT scores above 1100 (not including the writing section) or ACT scores above 20, and class rank in the top 25 percent. Most students don't do this well academically. Highly competitive colleges generally look for students in the top 5 percent of their class with a GPA of 3.75 or above. Even fewer students do this well. And even if you are within these ranges, you still may have trouble getting accepted, but at least you will be a contender. This doesn't mean these colleges won't accept students outside these ranges; it just means they aren't out actively *looking* for students outside these ranges.

If you are outside these ranges, don't worry. *Competitive colleges and highly competitive colleges, without exception, lower their academic standards when they find a student that has other characteristics they want.* The ideas in this book will help make *you* the student they want, even if your grades are pretty bad.

I speak from experience. I got into every competitive college I

---

6. Just because you haven't heard of a college doesn't mean it isn't a good college.

applied to, and I only had a 2.04 weighted GPA from high school and my SAT scores were just over 1000 (there was no writing test when I took the SAT). My academic record was not sexy. I was lucky that my parents loved me enough to think my poor academic performance would be fixed by sending me to a private school. It wasn't.

The most important thing to have right now is an honest-to-goodness desire to attend college. I don't care if you are motivated by a passion for learning or by the need to keep your parents happy.[7] If the desire is there, you will succeed. Whatever mistakes you have made up until this point can be fixed or at least replaced with new successes (unless your mistake landed you in prison).

CARROT:

For a list of competitive colleges, visit CollegePeas.com and enter the word COLLEGES in the CARROT Box.

Why You Are So Hard to Find

One of the main ways colleges try to find you is by renting your name from mailing list companies and sending you brochures and catalogs in hopes that their message will break through the clutter. There is a lot of clutter. In fact, you may already be getting reams of this material in your mailbox and in your e-mail inbox. When you take a standardized test, fill out a college research survey in school, or sign up to create a profile for colleges, you are likely to be added to a mailing list which is then sold to colleges and other companies out the back door for a tidy profit.

---

7. My parents were very education oriented. Even now it is difficult to unwind my desire for success from my desire to please my parents.

When a college rents your name, they refer to you as a "prospect." When a college sends you mail, they are trying to get you to respond and tell them you are interested. When you do respond to them, they add you to their internal mailing list and call you an "inquiry." Inquiries are students who have expressed interest in a particular college and have at least some interest in applying. Once you become an inquiry, it's the college's job to make sure you have the information you need and convince you to become an "applicant." An applicant is a student who has submitted a complete application for admission. Once you become an applicant, it's the college's job to send you a rejection or an acceptance letter. Once you become an accepted applicant, it's the college's job to get you to accept their offer and to collect your deposit. Once they collect your deposit, it's the college's job to make sure you show up on the first day of class—they now call you a "student." Once you become a student, it's *your* job to study for four years and graduate. Whew! College marketing is hard!

As you might imagine, it takes a lot of prospects to get one new student. It's expensive to send mail, so colleges limit their mailing efforts to areas of the country where they will get the biggest response. If you are in their region, for instance, you probably receive mail from them. The bad news is that there are lots of great colleges that simply can't reach you because you don't live in an area that they can afford to target.

Understanding Your Chances

When the dean of admissions at a competitive college sits down with her mocha latte and a stack of applications from hopeful students, she will be looking for students who will continue to make her campus the great college it is today. She needs to pick the students who will get involved on campus, make good grades, graduate, and become successful, supportive alumni.

Some of her choices are easy. There are a handful of applicants who are so outstanding that she sticks them in the "In" pile right away. These students had a 100-percent chance of getting in. There are also a lot of applicants whose credentials are so poor that she feeds them to her pet goat right away. These students had a 100-percent chance of getting rejected.

However, there is a sometimes-large pool of students in the middle where she has to think a little harder. If she has done her job well, she has narrowed the pool to a list that can easily allow her to meet her enrollment goals and then some. Imagine these students have about a fifty-fifty chance of being accepted, which means it contains twice as many students as she will need to meet her goal. These students are the "Maybes," and the dean will now have to do some work to decide if the application will go into the "In" folder or into the goat's belly. The more competitive her college is, the more Maybes she will have because fewer applicants will get stuck in the "In" folder right away.

What is most interesting about the Maybes is that she actually *wants* to accept all of them, but she can't. Most competitive colleges *want* to accept more applicants than they actually *do* accept. Remember, if they don't want you, they reject you—simple as that. But if they *do* want you, they may still reject you. If you are an average student, you need to convince the dean of admissions to accept you over other students they also want. This book can help.

I recently spoke to the dean of admissions at a competitive college who said his college sends rejection letters to the students they definitely don't want, and they send acceptance letters to those they definitely do want. They also send acceptance letters to the Maybes when they make it into the "In" folder. The rest of the Maybes receive *nothing at all.* The college never contacts them with a decision! He said that they let those "die on the vine." If one of those no-letter Maybes gives the college a call, they will pluck them off the vine and stick them in the "In" stack. It is a way for the students to self-select. It may sound weird, but it works for them!

The reason competitive colleges wind up rejecting students they want is because they are faced with the fact that they don't have enough room for all the students they would like to admit. Colleges are restricted by all sorts of things, ranging from the number of faculty members to the number of dorm rooms on campus. Sometimes these restraints can be lifted by hiring more faculty and administrators or building new buildings (colleges are constantly raising money so they can acquire these things), but it's not always possible. It's not always wanted either; being competitive in the first place is an important part of their draw and reputation.

If you are a 4.0-GPA student, valedictorian, president of the senior class, captain of the football team, regular volunteer at a homeless shelter, and have internship experience with a bio-medical research lab, you probably have a 100-percent chance of getting in for all but the most competitive colleges. If, on the other hand, you are a 2.0-GPA student with no sports, activities, jobs, or interests, you probably have a 100-percent chance

THE 100% NO GROUP

of becoming goat fodder for all but the least competitive colleges. There are lots of students in between, and lots of them are on the list of Maybes. It is from this list that colleges accept or reject applicants based on how they feel about your potential as a student rather than the cold, hard facts and numbers. When you are in this stack, the college is forced to take a more holistic approach to admissions and read applications more carefully. They are looking for a deeper understanding of who you are as a person and whether they think you will be happy and successful on their campus.

So what everybody wants to know is: how do these admissions people make up their minds?

It would be nice to know the answer to this question *before* you apply, but most competitive schools don't publish their admissions criteria. They do this for a number of reasons. The main reason is that the admissions process is far too nuanced to actually have an easily described admissions policy.

I once took a class in "decision science" where the professor described some of his research in admissions. The professor had designed a statistical model that would predict academic success based on application data. The model consistently beat the traditional admissions process by a very significant margin. He concluded that letting a computer program pick applicants was more accurate than humans. This is a revolutionary discovery. This means every college can fire their admissions staff and instead allow a computer model to do admissions for them. The only staff they would need is an administrative assistant to stuff the acceptance letters into envelopes and lick the stamps and a goat to eat all the rejected applications. There's only one catch:

accuracy in predicting academic success is *not* the goal of admissions counselors.

The goal of admissions is to recruit just the right number of smart students, athletic students, deep students, shallow students, political students, science students, teaching students, black students, white students, male students, foreign students, cute students, ugly students, nice students, hippie students, Republican students, funny students, weird students, uptight students, laid-back students, and the list goes on. Academic success isn't the only factor. It is a really important factor, but it isn't the only one. The important thing is creating a diverse student body who can introduce each other to a multitude of new ideas, opinions, and perspectives. The best educational experience happens when a diverse group of people hashes out an issue until they all have a better understanding of the issue and a better understanding of each other. If this were not the case, then we could all just buy the textbook and learn all we need to know.

Keeping You in the Dark

It would be nice if colleges would publish their admissions criteria on their websites[8] but, unfortunately for you, competitive colleges have to keep you in the dark. If a competitive college actually published its admissions criteria, then students could easily self-select. The 100-percent goat fodder people wouldn't apply in the first place. Only those who were in the 100-percent "In" group would bother applying. All of a sudden the college would look a whole lot less competitive.

Not all colleges say they care about looking competitive; they

---

8. Some actually do.

actually have a much bigger problem that has to do with the complexity of the process itself. Even if they could define admissions criteria, the act itself would limit their ability to find students. Imagine that you were asked to define the perfect friend and that you could only consider being friends with those who fit your description. Never mind that you would look like a jerk, but you would probably never meet some great people because they didn't fit your description. Sometimes you can tell within a few minutes of meeting someone if you are going to hit it off, but sometimes you have to look more carefully. You have to keep your options open, but always be mindful of your personal bandwidth. How likely are you to maintain close friendships with people who don't speak the same language as you? While it's not impossible that you would become friends, you have to focus on those who might be more compatible. So, you might picture what the perfect friend might be, but you have to keep it to yourself because you may alienate some prime candidates. Colleges deal with this kind of problem all the time.

I recently had a discussion with one of the admissions counselors from a top-five college. I asked her point-blank if there was a combination of grades and test scores that would eliminate a student from consideration and she said, "None; we like to consider every applicant." Hmm, I find it pretty hard to believe that a top-five college would even bother looking at an application that had a 2.0 GPA. I guess they would "consider" it long enough to read the GPA and stick in the shredder. The admissions counselor was quite nice, and I know she really wanted to reach out to *all* interested students, but the fact remains that there is no way that top colleges can *seriously* consider all applicants. There has to be some sort of cut off that will allow them to prioritize their time. And there are, but they are guidelines rather than rules.

Many colleges publish their historical admissions profiles in a document called the "Common Data Set," which is a standardized format that allows a college to deliver a complete organizational profile to publishers of college guides. Colleges often post their Common Data Set on their websites. According to the 2006–07 Common Data Set for the competitive college I spoke to that said they considered all applicants, not a single student from the bottom half of their graduating class was admitted.

CARROT: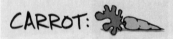

For more information about Common Data Sets, visit CollegePeas.com and enter CDS in the CARROT Box.

The information in the Common Data Set isn't the same thing as admissions criteria. When a college publishes actual criteria, it means that if you meet the criteria, you are in—simple as that. A college that is less competitive will be more likely to publish their admissions criteria. They will be more cut-and-dried and they will make fewer decisions based on their intuition. Less competitive colleges have a matrix that gives more cut-and-dry requirements for an in/out decision. They find you on the matrix and it will tell them if you are in or out.

It is not uncommon for community colleges or large state colleges to publish entrance criteria. It is much easier to check a few boxes than it is to pore over thousands of applications. The criteria aren't the same for everyone; for instance, the criteria for an in-state student are probably different than for an out-of-state student. Many state colleges have much lower admissions requirements for in-state students. (At the time I attended the University of Kansas, everyone who graduated from a high school in Kansas was admitted.)

CARROT:

To see a sample admissions matrix, visit CollegePeas.com and enter the word MATRIX in the CARROT Box.

Figuring Out Where You Stand

In spite of the fact that most competitive colleges don't publish their admissions criteria, you can still assess your own chances of getting in by doing a little research, asking some experts, and checking out the college's Common Data Set. You can compare your academic, personal, and extracurricular stats to the Common Data Set. Comparing your credentials to the averages published in the Common Data Set will let you know if you are above or below average. If you are way above average, you might be a good prospect for that college (duh). If you are below the average, you may still have a shot, but you will have to show the college that you are truly a person worth admitting *in spite* of your academic achievement. No college wants to admit a student who can't handle the work, but most colleges are willing to take a chance if they think you are a diamond in the rough. There is a lot of information to comb through, but I encourage you to do it if you have the time. However, if your academics are average or below average, you may have a harder time assessing your chances. In all cases it's a good idea to consult your guidance counselors, alumni of the college, and college admissions counselors (aka "The Gatekeepers").

If you can't find the college's Common Data Set, don't sweat it. The Internet is awash with college profile databases, and many of them are based on the Common Data Set. Much of this information comes from the government and is compiled so Uncle Sam can monitor educational statistics in the United States and in some cases keep track of colleges that offer federal financial aid.

Be advised, college admissions counselors will rarely tell you if they think you have a good or bad chance of getting in. They hate it when people try to assess their chances and cringe when students ask. They simply answer, "I'll have to look at your application first." They can, however, tell you about their freshman class profile so you can get a feel for where you stand. If you can convince them you're in the ballpark, they'll read your application and will inform you if you are in or out.

Making Your Move

However you assess your chances, you will derive one of three answers: 1) that you're close to a shoo-in, 2) that you're goat fodder, and 3) that you are a Maybe. If you are close to a shoo-in, this book will help you avoid any possible doubt. If you are a Maybe, then keep reading. If you are a no way, you might consider choosing a different college; you can apply if you are ready for the rejection letter.

College admissions counselors love it when people apply and

hate it when they are convinced not to apply. I believe that where there is a will there is a way. If you really want to go to a particular college for which you are underqualified, you can find a way.[9] However, I urge you not to get your heart set on one specific college. There are simply too many good colleges out there to choose from. On the average, it is virtually impossible to determine which college in the United States provides the "best" education. Don't beat a dead horse—there are lots of great colleges that you can get into. Remember, "best" really only has meaning in the context of the student being educated. A college filled with straight-A students may not be the right place for an average student.

If, after doing your research, you determine that you are a contender for a competitive school, it's now time to get your ducks in a row. The next few chapters will give you the secrets of success.

---

9. If you don't believe me, try watching the movie *Rudy* about a kid's dream to attend Notre Dame.

Chapter 2

THE GATEKEEPERS—WHO ARE THESE PEOPLE WHO DETERMINE YOUR FATE?

Before we get to specific tactics, you need to understand the landscape of college admissions and who the key players are. You can't get into college if you are an island—you have to interact (positively) with others. The people you come in contact with during your college search will make the difference for you. They can destroy an otherwise good candidate's chances and radically improve an otherwise poor candidate's chances.

A college student represents tens of thousands of dollars in college revenue over the next four to six years.[10] It is not uncommon for a college education to cost well over $100,000. This is real money that a college actually receives on your behalf. You may

---

10. Most college students take more than four years to graduate from college. I personally took five years and two summers to get my bachelor's degree. You do have to pay for the extra time, so this is only a financial problem because staying in college as long as possible can be a blast.

not actually pay the money up front, but rest assured that the money changes hands whether it comes from you, your parents, your grandparents, your bank, your government, your scholarship provider, or from the college's endowment funds in the form of scholarships and grants. Your tuition *must* get paid. Education is the product, you are the buyer, and the college is the seller. Next to medicine, education (including college) is the largest industry in the United States—we're talking big money and high stakes.

What you may (or may not) find interesting is that this high-value, high-stakes industry is dominated by government entities and non-profit organizations.[11] High schools are usually government-funded institutions often called "public" schools or they can be non-profit entities often called "private" schools (although some private schools are actually run as for-profit businesses). A college is usually either a government-run institution (public college, often called a "state" college) or a non-profit business (private college). There is a third player in the equation: the for-profit college (often called a career college or a proprietary college). Still, non-profit and government colleges dominate the industry and set the tone. When most people talk about college admissions, they are talking about a high school student from a public or private high school trying to get admitted into a public or private college. *All* competitive colleges are either public or private non-profit institutions. None of them are proprietary. However, that doesn't mean there aren't proprietary colleges out there that can offer you the education you want; it just means they have high acceptance rates.

During the process, you will encounter people who make a living as college admissions professionals. These people are the

---

11. Bureaucrats and hippies make for an interesting system.

Gatekeepers. They are also known as guidance counselors or college counselors on the high school side and college admissions counselors on the college side.

Before we go any further, let me make something clear about Gatekeepers: their job is to help you find the right education. They are there to help you, and you can't do it on your own. I reiterate: you *cannot* get accepted to a competitive college (or any college) without working with these people. If you respect them you will do better than if you don't. If you admire them, you will do even better. These people come in different forms. Let's take a look at who they are.

High School Counselors

A high school counselor helps students figure out how to get through high school and in some cases, transition to college. While many counselors have master's degrees in education and counseling, there are few, if any, programs that teach college counseling. So your counselor probably learned on the job. They learned by speaking with kids, parents, and admissions counselors and attending professional meetings like those sponsored by the National Association for College Admissions Counseling (NACAC).

A high school counselor is a Gatekeeper in the sense that he or she has the power to convince you or dissuade you from applying to a college in the first place. But they have no real power when it comes to whether or not you will be accepted. Some of the top ones may be able to go out on a limb with some of their admissions counterparts at different colleges or at least get them to listen, but don't count on it. The good ones don't play games with their own reputation. They will try and represent you fairly and accurately to colleges. They will *not* exaggerate your qualifications, but they will highlight and/or downplay certain aspects of your qualifications to make the best case. For instance, if you are a great tuba player but a lousy basketball player, your guidance counselor will highlight your musical talent and avoid discussion of your athletic prowess.

In most cases, your high school counselor can help you determine which schools might be a good fit for you. There is probably nobody else you know who has visited more colleges, talked to more admissions counselors, or read more college catalogs than high school counselors. Do not hesitate to pick their brains about specific colleges. They will also be able to help you generate some ideas for where you might be a good fit. They may not know you very well, so it is your job to help them become familiar with who you are. They see gazillions of kids, and most of the kids are just like you.

If you aren't a top student, you may feel that it's hard to get time with your counselor. This is not true. Make an appointment, show up, and become your own advocate. You are the captain of your application team, and your guidance counselor is your quarterback. Make sure you have a game plan, and take responsibility for making it happen. Counselors are there to help, they want to help, and they, more than anyone, can help. You just need to ask for it and do your part.

One thing is true about high school counselors: the vast majority of them have more work than one person can handle effectively. The average public high school counselor serves over three hundred students. The worst situation is in California, where those poor souls can be responsible for over one thousand students each!

Being an overworked high school counselor isn't a problem for high school counselors. They are professionals, and they manage their overload by concentrating on the kids they need to concentrate on. They may seem to be either ignoring you or just going through the motions so they don't get a call from your annoying parents who think they can actually *get you into* a given college (they can't). Even if your parents don't nag them to death, they have a million other things occupying their time.

These people are pushed hard by the administration, and their responsibilities often include things other than getting you into college. At the same time they are working on college admissions, they are dealing with teen pregnancies, drug problems, disciplinary problems, child abuse, and a whole host of other problems that find their way into the counseling office. They have to manage all these other responsibilities in addition to helping kids apply to college. To make matters worse, some of them have to process lots of applications because their students are so afraid they won't get accepted that they want to submit an application to every college they can think of (a silly waste of time).

If your high school counselor is one of the plethora of counselors who are overworked, you will have to work around the problem. It may not be your fault, but it is your problem. It's your problem because they are not totally focused on you and are not likely to focus on you any time soon. If you really want their attention, either be a hotshot with perfect grades and a winning season or do some of the things in this book. Your guidance counselor *wants* to help you, but you probably aren't helping them help you. You will be surprised to see these busy people take time for you if you simply ask. And as long as you don't waste their time by being unprepared or uninterested, they will continue to make time to work on your case.

Independent Counselors

If you can afford it, you might consider hiring an independent college counselor. These people are generally former high school counselors or college admissions counselors. These people sometimes *do* make promises about getting you in. If you find one that is making such a claim, drop them like a hot potato. These counselors can't get you in any more than your high school counselor can. What they can do is help you whip your essays in shape and keep you on schedule. If you engage them early in your high school career, they can help shape your academic and extracurricular choices. They can help you pick classes, develop your interests, and even find a tutor if you are having trouble. They can't really come in at the last minute and get you into a competitive college, but they can make a positive impact if given enough time. Independent counselors are great if your high school counselor simply can't provide you the time you need to prepare for college.

There are lots of independent counselors around because high school counselor and college admissions counselor jobs typically don't pay very well and carry with them a bunch of headaches that most people would rather live without. Many high school counselors and admissions counselors love to do college counseling, and they think that going out on their own and doing just college counseling is a good idea. As an independent counselor, they can pick their own hours, be their own boss, and in some cases make as much or more money than they did before.

If you do work with an independent counselor, remember that they *do not* replace your high school counselor. You still need to work with your high school counselor because if a college wants to verify information about you or your application, they will call your high school counselor, not your independent counselor. Good high school counselors will be charming and helpful on the call, but some may see your engagement with an independent counselor as a personal insult and let it come across in a phone call with the college. Some independent counselors get a bad rap from the industry. I think they can be a good investment, and most of them really enjoy their work. Just to be safe, keep your relationship with your independent counselor on the down-low with your high school and with colleges.

Another danger of working with an independent counselor is that you run the risk of looking "packaged." A packaged application is one that is so neatly put together that it looks like an independent counselor put it together. Colleges hate this. Applications like this lack personality and authenticity. The good independent counselors know this and will be careful not to over-influence the process. If you feel at all uncomfortable with your final application, it may be because it doesn't reflect your true self. While it should certainly reflect your best self, it must also reflect your true self. If you feel your independent counselor may have packaged your application, you may get this feeling. Do not hesitate to bounce it off a few other people. I recommend asking your guidance counselor and some of your references to take a look. They will tell you what you might do to make it more authentic.

College admissions deans and counselors can smell a packaged application; it's kind of like that "new car" smell.

College Admissions Deans and Counselors

College admissions deans and counselors, unlike high school counselors, actually *do* have the power to get you into a particular college. They can, within reason, admit anyone they want. If the dean of admissions of a competitive college lets in a student with a 2.0 GPA, they may have some explaining to do, but (and here is the kicker) if the dean can tell a good story, then there is no problem. Ta-da! The 2.0 student gets in. A good story is a unique story.

Often budding admissions counselors get their start while they are in college themselves by giving campus tours to college hopefuls. They make friends with the admissions office staff and as graduation day grows closer, they realize their job prospects are dim and/or they realize that getting paid while hanging around a college campus for another few years is actually a sweet gig. So, they tell the existing dean that they want to work in the admissions office full-time. The dean will either hire them or make a few calls and convince a buddy at a different college to hire them.

From there they are put on the road to "work their territory," where they will schmooze hundreds, if not thousands, of college hopefuls like you. It is unlikely they will remember you. They can't remember everyone they meet. There are too many cities, too many college fairs, and too many kids. They don't remember most of the people they speak to. It is your job to make sure they remember you by reminding them over and over that you want to go to their college. By following the advice in this book, you will have a few things that will make you worth remembering.

If you apply to a smaller liberal arts school, your application will probably be assigned to an individual counselor who will be your point person. Get their e-mail address and cell phone number. Call them whenever you have a question and follow up on everything you or anyone else sends them. The more you call, the more likely they are to remember you when it comes to sorting out the wheat from the chaff. There is a fine line between keeping yourself on the radar screen and being annoying. Make sure you have a substantive issue to discuss when you call. Don't just call to say hello or check in. This may not be practical at a large school or a state school, but try calling anyway. Admissions departments often track these interactions.

Like high school guidance counselors, admissions counselors also have more work than they can reasonably be expected to handle. So, like high school counselors, they pick the kids who are clearly strong candidates who will actually enroll if they are accepted. Most of the time they can tell with a quick glance at the student's GPA and test scores: top students get in,[12] bottom students get rejected, and they set aside those who are in the middle so they can read them later—the Maybes.

If you are an admissions dean, you are under enormous pressure from the college's administration to deliver your enrollment goal for the year. If you are short even a few people, the impact can be devastating. As mentioned earlier, each student is worth thousands of dollars. If the incoming class is short ten to twenty students, it could mean a loss of a million dollars or more. On

---

12. Only a highly competitive school would consider rejecting a top student with solid test scores.

the flip side of the coin, if too many students enroll, the college will be over capacity and they will need to find extra dorm rooms, extra seats, open more classes, etc., at a potential cost of thousands of dollars. Admissions is a tightrope, and the admissions dean has a powerful tool to ensure he or she doesn't fall short or go over. It's called a waitlist, and it's filled with the Maybes that didn't turn into "definitelys" (in or out).

By the way, it takes years and years for an admissions professional to develop the skills necessary to meet the enrollment goals for a competitive college. When you speak to the dean of admissions, you are speaking with a person with extremely well-developed skills and experience. It is very difficult to obtain a top admissions position at a competitive college. Respect these people!

Your Parents

There is another group of people who have direct impact on the college admissions process: your parents. Many parents feel that their success as a parent is wrapped up in your ability to get into the right college. For the first time their little baby is being formally judged by people other than them. Sure, your teachers gave you grades, but it's not the same. In this case, they think your life is on the line!

Some parents complicate the matter by imposing their viewpoints and pressures on you, the hapless applicant. I have pictures from my childhood wearing Harvard T-shirts. I was about two years old, and my parents were already setting college expectations!

The best thing your parents can do is to help you complete your application, watch your butt so you don't miss deadlines, show you the love and support you deserve as you make this emotionally charged transition, and of course, support your decision. The *worst* thing they can do is to become overly involved in your college application process or actually make contact with anyone on your behalf. They can talk to your high school counselor but should not talk on your behalf. They should never, ever lobby to a college admissions department unless they have had a campus building named after them. Even then it's risky. Never let your parents complete your application or (gasp) write your essay for you. Admissions counselors can almost always tell when this happens, and goats love the taste of your parents' essays.

I recently volunteered to represent my alma mater at a local college fair. The best parents stood back while their kids did the talking. They didn't ask questions but listened carefully to the questions their kids asked and the answers I gave. Even when I tried to engage the parents directly, they deferred to their child. This is good—really good. One parent, however, talked to me in detail about her daughter's busy schedule and how she had been unable to get in touch with the right people in admissions. When I asked her where her daughter was, the mother told me she was at home. This is bad—really bad. This parent was really hurting her daughter's chances of finding the right college. Her intentions were great, but her daughter, busy or not, should have been the one calling the admissions department and visiting college fairs. Bottom line: no matter how good your parents' intentions are, if they do your work during the college admissions process, they will not only annoy the admissions office, but also they will make you look like an immature baby.

Your parents can be an important part of the process as long as they play a behind-the-scenes role. They play the role of cheering

fans. When it comes to college visits, try to take your parents with you whenever possible. They will probably be paying for it and will appreciate being included. More importantly, however, they know you better than anyone and they can help you assess how good a fit the college might be. They can stroll around the campus while you are in your interview and take a look at the town.

Do not take them to your interview and do not take them to any organized events, unless they are specifically invited. You are in charge of this experience, not your parents. Admissions counselors want to see a kid who can take care of him or herself. Explain to your parents, in advance, that you need to do these things on your own but that you do want their opinion. Buy them a copy of this book to read while they wait.[13] If the admissions counselor has decided they want you to attend their college, they will do everything in their power to ensure you enroll. This often includes contacting your parents directly and selling them on the opportunity. This is okay. If you've reached this point, you have a good chance of being accepted.

If you find yourself in an awkward situation, such as bumping into the admissions counselor in the cafeteria and having your parents invite him or her to join you, make sure you do most of the talking. This is your program, and you need to maintain control. If you are a choice candidate for the college, the counselor will try and sell you and your parents on the college. If you are not a choice candidate, you will have to show them that you are a responsible and independent person.

Note to parents reading this book: please re-read the above section and discuss it with your kids. It is

---

13. Do not loan them this book unless you are pretty sure they will lose it and have to buy another copy. The more copies that people buy, the better life will be for me.

very important that you take a cheerleader role in this process and let your kid take the driver's seat. Even if your kids beg you to take the lead for them, you have to back off. If you ever have the urge to butt in and take control of the college application process, find a distraction as soon as possible.

Chapter 3

SIGNIFICANTLY INCREASE YOUR CHANCES OF GETTING IN

Unless you are certain you're in the 100-percent chance of getting in group, you probably run the risk of falling into the Maybe stack. The following technique is the most important thing you can do to "write your own ticket" to the front of the line. First, you must realize that you have a problem. The problem is that you are a teenager and most adults can't tell one teenager from another unless they already know you well. Most admissions professionals are adults. So, you need to do something to break away from the pack.

Adults vs. Teenagers

For the purposes of this discussion, a teenager is a person who is thirteen to twenty-two[14] years old and is either on their way to college or is already in college. An adult is someone who has 1) completed puberty and 2) pays their own bills. The difference has nothing to do with maturity level.

Here is why adults can't tell one teenager from another. Unlike other demographic groups, teenagers are far more influenced by their peers than they are by those who are older or younger than them.[15] Peer influence is so powerful at this age that teenage consumption habits are even consistent across cultures. This means teenagers buy almost the same clothing, games, music, food, entertainment, and just about anything else they can think of whether they are from the United States, Japan, England, France, China—you name it. From an adult's perspective, every teenager looks identical to the next. Adults, on the other hand, are just as likely to be influenced by someone outside their peer group as those inside it. Adults are influenced by coworkers (who may be older or younger, married or unmarried, ugly or hot), parents, kids (even teenage kids), or just about anyone else with some seemingly good advice.

From a college admissions perspective, this is a nightmare. The college admissions professional is an adult and to the adult, most teenagers look the same. If you are a teenager, I'm sorry to tell you this, but I speak the truth. I'm sure it's no surprise to learn that

---

14. I realize that people twenty to twenty-two aren't technically teenagers, but they are for the purposes of this book.

15. There is only one other group who looks and acts more homogeneously than teenagers—the filthy rich. Wealthy people also tend to be influenced by each other rather than by non-wealthy people. They buy the same cars, houses, vacations, investments, and watches as other really wealthy people.

HOW ADULTS SEE TEENAGERS

you live in a world where nobody outside your peer group under-stands you! So how in the world do college admissions counselors tell the difference between you and every other teenage college applicant? The first thing they do is look at your GPA. Next they will look at your test scores.[16] In fact, in some cases they won't look past the cold, hard numbers on your transcript unless they absolutely have to. Never assume that they will read your essays or even glance at your letters of reference; most will, but don't count on it. Hopefully your grades and test scores are not so bad that they toss your application, laughing, into the 100-percent reject pile. Or, better yet, maybe you are so good that they can toss you into the 100-percent get-in pile. A quick gut-check on the rest of your application can seal your fate. If your GPA and test scores don't give them the quick-sort, they will be faced with the task of trying to discern one teenager from another—a task for which they, like any other adult, are ill equipped.

I'm sure this message is disconcerting. After all, most teen-agers would like to think of themselves as individuals. In fact, most of them spend most of their time trying to be individuals. Unfortunately, when viewed from outside the teenage world, you are in lockstep with every other teenager.

There is, however, a very powerful way to differentiate yourself from other teenagers. It is simple, it works, and it is your biggest opportunity when it comes to college admissions.

Non-Teenager Activities—NTAs

Here it is: do something that most teenagers don't do. If you want a *serious* edge when applying to college, engage in an activity that

---

16. Some colleges are "test-optional," which means you have the option of not showing them your test scores. They will look at your grades and class rank and, in most cases, they will look at your test scores too if you submit them.

only an adult would do. I call this a Non-Teenager Activity or NTA. If you can do this, can do it early, and can do it even sort of well, you will *always* beat the odds. NTAs can include just about anything you or your peer group does not currently do. Take quilting, for example; I'll bet most teenagers don't quilt, nor do they know other teenagers who quilt. If you learn to quilt (sort of well) and send your college admissions counselor a picture of you donating your quilts to needy families, you will shine in their eyes.

NTAs—Making Them Work

Doing an NTA is probably the quickest, most effective thing you can do to differentiate yourself from other teenagers.[17] When it comes to college admissions, if you engage in an NTA, it will separate you and allow you to relate better to adults, which is what you are ultimately trying to do—convince an adult to let you into their college. And it is much easier than it sounds (even if your grades are weak)—just pick something that you wouldn't normally consider doing.

Engaging in an NTA is best for students who start a few years before their application is due. It would be hard to cram a meaningful NTA in a month before the deadline, but if you think you can, go for it.

I was a pretty bad student who stumbled upon several things that gave me an admissions edge. One of these things was engaging in an NTA. When I was in high school, I raised homing pigeons. This may sound like a silly way to spend your time as

---

17. By the way, I'm not saying there is anything wrong with teenagers; I'm saying that, as a group, you are difficult to understand by non-teenagers. You know this already, I know you do.

a teenager (and it may have been), but it really got me noticed by colleges. If it weren't for those silly birds, I would have been a *nothing* in the college admissions process. I had terrible grades in high school and mediocre test scores. I didn't even realize that my school offered AP classes, and I pretty much sucked at sports (keep this in mind for a later story).

But, unlike most other teenagers, I raised and trained homing pigeons. When I actually brought a homing pigeon to a college interview and released it with a note attached, I was impossible to forget. The admissions counselor would look past my lousy application and look in amazement as he or she watched the bird fly off into the heavens only to arrive safely at my home several hours or days later. It was a sight to see and, as a result, I had a *serious* edge over applicants who were much more academically qualified than I was. My friends (and yes, I did have friends), thought my birds were sort of cool, but nobody was interested enough to raise pigeons with me.

I started raising homing pigeons in grade school at the encouragement of a friend's father who thought my friend and I could send messages back and forth because we lived several towns apart. I liked the idea and found a guy (an adult) who had some birds. He showed me what to do, and in no time I had converted our shed into a pigeon coop. My friend never did it, but I raised a small flock and I took care of them for five or six years until I went to college, when my dad took over.[18] They are called homing pigeons because they don't leave! I was actually *forced* to take care of these critters through high school whether I liked it or not.

I also did many teenager things like surfing, skateboarding, yearbook, school magazine, and sports, which are all great things.

---

18. My homing pigeon hobby came to an end when my parents sold our house—the birds never left!

FINDING AN NTA

But to an admissions counselor they sound a lot like "blah, blah, blah, and blah." This is not to say that there is anything wrong with surfing, skateboarding, yearbook, school magazine, and sports, and I encourage you to do whatever it is you enjoy, but they will not help you stand out among your peers. I accidentally stumbled upon this little gem—but you can proactively engage in such an activity, and I promise it will give you an edge.

I, the terrible, boring student, got a serious edge in the college admissions process because I was actively engaged in an NTA. The moral of the story is that admissions counselors don't need another mediocre student who does sports and helps on the yearbook. What they do need is a quirky kid who releases homing pigeons during their college interviews.

Spotting an NTA

NTAs aren't your run-of-the-mill activities. Participating on your school's yearbook staff, for instance, is not an NTA. In fact, teenagers put every high school yearbook in the world together. It's a good learning experience, and I encourage you to do it, but it won't necessarily help you stand out—regardless of what your parents, teachers, or guidance counselors tell you. Do the yearbook, but also do an NTA.

Managing the yearbook staff, on the other hand, is more of an NTA. Because many adults tend to view teenagers as wild animals who travel in packs, a leader seems less like a teenager. Thus, leadership experience means a whole lot more than simply being part of the pack. This applies to everything, so be a leader or at least act like a leader (adults can't tell the difference between an actual leader and someone who merely acts like a leader). To take it one step further, *running* a yearbook business is a very non-teenager thing to do and will easily help you stand out from the crowd. Few teenagers, if any, own yearbook production companies. We'll explore some other examples in the next chapter, but let's take a moment to show how your NTA can get you noticed.

Getting Noticed

Once you get an NTA, you will be able to promote yourself to colleges in a variety of ways. First, it will be the topic of at least one of your essays (the optional essay). If your grades and test scores are weak, your application essays may not be read very carefully or possibly not at all, so you will need to make sure your guidance counselor and references are well-informed so they can make contact with the admissions department on your behalf and highlight your NTA (more later on this).

However, you must understand that your goal is not to simply get noticed. Just because you get noticed doesn't make it right. In the spring of 2007, the *Wall Street Journal* ran an article about college admissions.[19] The article was about how colleges are rejecting students in record numbers. The article mentioned a guy who camped out in front of the admissions department because he wanted to be noticed. He was, indeed, noticed, but it did not help him stand out among his peers. Why? Simple—it was not an NTA. In fact, nobody who isn't a teenager would consider such a stunt. The teenager thought it would be a great way to show his interest in the school. But remember, college admissions counselors (adults) don't understand teenage behavior and thus don't

---

19. It is called "Students Play the Waitlist Game," April 11, 2007.

understand why someone would camp out in front of their office. We discussed this topic with Scott Friedhoff, VP for Enrollment at Allegheny College. Scott did not recommend doing this. Scott, like many adults, thought this was foolish behavior. A better idea would have been for the guy to start an admissions road trip club with fifty students traveling from college to college to see their campuses. Camping out is a teenager activity; creating an organization that promotes the importance of visiting colleges is an NTA. Scott would have been impressed.

Engaging in an NTA isn't about padding your resume. Anyone in college admissions can tell the difference between a real NTA and a resume-builder. NTAs are about exploring activities outside your immediate comfort zone and embracing them. One good NTA will outshine a list of resume-building teenager activities any day of the week.

Leadership

The idea that teenagers run in packs is a common sentiment among adults. We can hardly tell one from the other. Some of us consider teenagers downright dangerous and we avoid them at all costs. (Not me. I love you guys!) So, like I mentioned before, leadership is important.

There are three types of leadership. The first type is being appointed or elected to be a leader. An appointed or elected leader would be class president, team captain, or store manager. The next type of leader is a talent leader. Talent leaders are All-American goalies, the winner of the state championship in debate,[20] or a

---

20. Winning a state championship is not an NTA. Only teenagers win state championships. Having the talent to win a state championship is an NTA.

wonderful musician. The last type of leader is a passion leader. This is a person who stands out because of their dedication or passion for a particular activity. I know a girl who played piano and studied ballet every day from the time she was three years old. She had passion and dedication.[21] Most teenagers don't show these kinds of traits, and hence it is an NTA. She also had talent leadership. She often took the lead spot in annual ballet recitals. This is another NTA. Her grades were marginal, but because of her NTA, she was accepted to a Big Ten university.

The problem with leadership is that it is difficult to put yourself in a position of leadership.[22] Being a basketball player is an unimpressive, teenager activity. Being a kick-butt, leading player, however, is a cool NTA. Most teenagers are not world-class athletes. Colleges snatch these people up as fast as they can. The same goes for the top musicians, actors, artists, writers, science geeks, etc. It's hard to be at the top, and you probably aren't there. The good news is that you can choose quilting or homing pigeons to have a similar impact. Yes, you read that right, choosing the right NTA can improve your chances of being admitted in the same way as being a great athlete. You may think you aren't in the same ballpark as the top baseball player in your school. But, your NTA may show just as much passion and commitment as they do. Just because you can hit a ball doesn't mean you can train a homing pigeon!

---

21. Never mind that her mother made her do this against her will, it still looks good to colleges.

22. If it were easy, everyone would do it.

Finding NTAs

Most of us think that a top athlete is a shoo-in to most colleges. This is true; colleges actively recruit these people because they understand the activity (top performance) as an NTA. (Again, I'm not suggesting that teenager activities are bad; I'm simply suggesting that it is nearly *impossible* for the adult to see the difference between teenagers unless they are engaged in an NTA.) The good news for you is that if you forgot to even exercise for three years of high school, you can still up your odds of being accepted to the college of your choice; you need to engage in an NTA that will put you in the same league. There are many.

First, ask yourself, what do adults do? And, what do teenagers *not* do? This may be trickier than it sounds. Most teenagers are so immersed in teenager activities that they are oblivious to the world around them. (Note: not being oblivious to the world around you is, in itself, an NTA and it will help you stand out!) You can spot an NTA based on the number of non-teenagers engaged in the activity. Earlier I used the example of quilting. Very few teenagers know how to quilt. Thus, it's an NTA. Quilting per-se is not going to give you as much of an edge as being the top basketball player in the country, but it will give you a huge edge over the other teenagers with track records comparable to yours. Other activities include:

- Build a sailboat from scratch
- Restore antique instruments
- Climb Mount Everest or Mount Everest, Jr.
- Discover and name a new star or planet

- Volunteer at a medical clinic in Africa and deliver babies[23]
- Breed a special strain of flower and name it after your dead grandmother
- Make a real movie and distribute it to real movie theaters
- Invent something
- Underwater basket weaving
- Become a TV or radio personality (*everybody* loves TV)
- Write articles for a local newspaper
- Help run a political campaign

These examples may seem like overly challenging engagements, but they may not be. Breeding plants may not be that hard. You may be able to buy some nice plans and instructions for building a boat. There are an infinite number of stars in the sky—how hard can it be to find one? You don't have to be an astronomer to look through a telescope and take notes. The fact that most people perceive these things as difficult will work to your advantage. Raising homing pigeons is pretty easy, but it seems complicated and time-consuming.

It's important to show that you are committed to your interests. A student with a single, powerful NTA is much more likely to stand out than the student with a bunch of typical, teenager interests. During the admissions committee review they will say, "Mike is that guy who brought a homing pigeon with him to the interview and let me write a note to send on its leg. It was great; the guy really knew what he was doing. He raises them and trains them to fly back. Mike called a few hours later and let me know that the pigeon had beat him home. Mike's an

23. My wife knows a guy who did this. He was only in high school, yet he spent a summer in Africa delivering babies. He is now a doctor.

interesting guy. His grades were a little lower than most of our students, but what passion!"

If you have a bunch of typical teenager activities they will say, "I don't remember speaking to that kid—did he come in for an interview? Yearbook? What?" There are over twenty-three thousand high schools in the United States. That means there are twenty-three thousand football captains, twenty-three thousand prom queens, and twenty-three thousand valedictorians. Admissions counselors simply can't tell one class president from another.

Get the picture?

CARROT: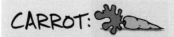

For a list of additional NTA ideas, visit CollegePeas.com and enter NTA in the CARROT Box.

Being Impressive

When you pick your NTA, make sure it looks hard, like breeding a special strain of flower. Read a few articles about genetics and be prepared to quote some of the concepts. Bring a flower to your interview, put a packet of seeds in your application envelope, and make it impressive. If you are really into it, then it will shine.

I recently heard a story of a student who collected cups of ice from fast food restaurants. She simply went in the door and asked for a cup of ice. She then went home, let the ice melt, and tested it for bacteria. She found lots of bacteria. So, she wrote up her findings and presented them to her city's health inspector, who ran it up the flagpole and some new laws got passed as a result. What a great NTA story!

Starting a Business

One of the easiest ways to engage in an impressive NTA is to start a business and make some money. Everybody loves money. You can give it away to charity or you can blow it on junk if you want, but be sure to put a little aside so the admissions counselor knows you're saving for college. Most teenagers don't start businesses, so it's ideal. Make sure it's a real business that has customers and if possible at least one real, non-teenager employee. Businesses are great because they show leadership skills (which comes in handy if you weren't popular enough to be elected class president), and they make you look like a responsible person.

If you start a business and are lucky enough to run into some problems, you can go to an adult for help, work through the problem, and have some real conversation starters during your interview. Successfully overcoming obstacles is the quickest way to being an impressive applicant. Make sure you write about your business in your essays and make sure your guidance counselor knows about it too so he or she can make a few calls on your behalf (don't assume colleges will read your essays). If you make something or sell something, you can bring a sample to your interview or mail a sample with your application—big points. Tip: products are generally more impactful than services because they are tangible. I applied to a highly competitive business school after college—a top-twenty program. Like high school, I had lousy grades, but I had started several businesses, one of which manufactured outdoor clothing. I plopped one of the jackets that I designed and my company manufactured down on the interviewer's desk. Think I got in?

Visuals are always great. Another great visual I had was a three-inch thick file folder filled with thank-you notes from happy customers. This is all good stuff. Run your business so you get thank-you notes, save them, photocopy them, and staple the copies to your optional essay about your NTA and providing good customer service.

Here are some examples of great businesses that you can start with fairly low upfront investments:

- [Justaboutanything].com
- Local services (painting, lawn mowing)
- Local newspaper
- Manufacture custom grill covers
- Printed sportswear
- Selling quilts, candles, or baskets

All of these things are real businesses that a teenager can start and thus be engaged in an NTA. It is important, however, that the business is a business and not just a part-time job. If you mow lawns, you don't have a lawn-mowing business. If you have ten people that you hire and pay to mow your customers' lawns and you own all the equipment because you saved last summer's lawn-mowing money to buy it, you have a business.

Starting a newspaper is easy. I started a local paper when I was still in grade school. I asked my classmates to write articles, and I sold ads to local businesses. The paper itself was actually pretty lame, and it only lasted a few issues, but I was lucky enough to run into a real problem: I didn't generate enough revenue from subscriptions and advertising to cover printing costs. I had to negotiate a deal with the school to use their copiers. Instead of bailing out, I solved the problem. Problems in your business are a gift; solve them and you will shine! If I had kept my newspaper going through high school, it would have been a *great* NTA.

Charities

A good, hard-hitting NTA doesn't have to be a hobby or business. A good, viable alternative to starting a business is to organize a charity. Charities are nice because they often require less structure, can be shorter term, and show that you have a great, big heart (remember, most adults fear teenagers).

Keep in mind, however, that *participating* in a charity is a teenager activity. Many, many teenagers participate in charities. Charities are good; charities teach you important lessons about life and help people, animals, or plants in need. Join them, love them, and support them. However, participating in a charity will not give you a big, fat, unfair advantage when it comes to getting into college.

Organizing a charity, however, will, especially if the charity raises money and is organized outside of any other formal organization. In other words, talking your Boy Scout troop into cleaning up the highway isn't the same thing as establishing a charity to clean up the highways with independent volunteers. For bonus points, make sure at least some of your volunteers aren't teenagers.

Bonus Chapter!

To read the bonus chapter about how Bacteria Girl beat the Valedictorian, visit CollegePeas.com and enter the word BACTERIA in the CARROT Box.

Turning a Teenager Activity into an NTA

Sometimes you can take a typical teenager activity and turn it into an NTA. Taking it to the next level is a good way. I know a girl who joined "Best Buddies" and became a friend to another girl who had terminal cancer. This is a teenager activity but not an NTA; it is great, but it may go largely unnoticed by admissions counselors who are used to seeing applicants participate in these types of programs all the time. (Again, don't get me wrong; Best Buddies is a great program, but I'm talking about NTAs that will give you a serious, unfair advantage over other applicants.)

The girl I know, however, created an NTA shortly after the friend she met through Best Buddies died. She started a charity in her friend's name selling stuffed kittens. She convinced a major toy company to donate the kittens and enlisted an army of volunteers to sell them all over town. The charity was a big hit, and she raised hundreds (maybe thousands) of dollars to fight cancer in her friend's name. Luckily for her, she ran into a major obstacle: she ran out of kittens! That didn't stop her—she is now actively soliciting local businesses to donate the cash for more kittens in exchange for some positive PR. Admissions counselors and deans will eat this up when she is ready to apply to college. This activity will give her an enormous advantage over other applicants with a similar or even better academic record. This is a great example of turning a teenager activity into an NTA. (Note: the army of volunteers she enlisted will not be engaged in an NTA. It's only an NTA for the founder and her partners. Many teenagers participate in charities; very few of them start charities.)

Charities are often easier to start than businesses because it can be easier to assemble a team of volunteers and convince people to donate. Hiring employees, paying taxes, selling products, etc., can be harder. However, they are not always easier to start and often require a much higher emotional commitment than most people are willing to make. You need to really care about your cause to dedicate the time and energy to following through. You don't really have to care that much about grass to mow lawns—earning money is the motivation. So, there are pros and cons for each. If you have a cause, start a charity; if you don't, start a business.

Keep it Real

Just because you have an NTA on your application doesn't mean it's going to help (even if it gets you noticed). Your NTA has to be real and substantiated. When you describe your NTA, make sure you are straightforward and honest. If you want your NTA to sound impressive, make sure it *is* impressive. Admissions counselors don't have time for people who puff up their accomplishments to look better than they really are. While it's not uncommon for people to get overly excited about their projects, you should be able to back up your claims with reality.

I ran into this trouble inadvertently when I applied to college. I nipped it in the bud before it got out of hand, but it could have quickly made me appear to be dishonest (even though I wasn't). On paper, I appeared to have a great NTA—sports. I told the truth on my application, but the facts didn't reflect reality, and it could have come back to bite me.

When I was in fourth grade, my school had a lacrosse team. I was a newly imported transplant from Kansas to the East coast, and I had never even heard of lacrosse. I went out for the team, and I was instantly proven to be a disgrace to the game! Luckily for me, my school had a policy that *all* kids had to play a sport, and thus, I couldn't get cut from the team. I loved lacrosse and when I went to high school, I wound up on the varsity team all four years. I had nine years of experience playing lacrosse with four years on varsity. This was pretty impressive. Most colleges were lucky if they could find a student with a couple of years of varsity play.

This was all true. I did play lacrosse for nine years, and I did play varsity for four years in high school. However, this is not the whole story. My high school started the lacrosse team the year I arrived. Any student who tried out was put on the team, even beginners. In spite of my long lacrosse career, I never actually got good at lacrosse. I just felt like playing. In all nine years, I only scored one goal. One goal in nine years!

About a week after my application was mailed out, I began to get excited calls from coaches. One, from a competitive school in Ohio, wanted to fly me out to meet the team. He gave me verbal acceptance to the school over the phone and promised a four-year scholarship that would have covered more than half my tuition. I thanked him and then politely declined his offer. He was pretty upset that I wasn't even willing to visit, but I explained to him that I only looked good on paper and I wasn't interested in pursuing the sport in college.[24] Even after I explained the situation, he was still interested in meeting me, but I knew I wouldn't be able to live up to his expectations.

I told the truth on my application, and it was misinterpreted as an NTA. Sports leadership like this is rare. However, because the

---

24. I actually did play one season in college as a club sport. Also, I coached lacrosse years later and one of the other coaches introduced me to a hot chick who eventually became my wife. Lacrosse is a great sport.

facts didn't shine through, I actually alienated some good colleges because I couldn't back up the claims. It was an accident; I didn't know better. Don't put yourself in this position. Make sure you are clear about your accomplishments. I got accepted, but for the wrong reasons.

At the end of the day, colleges want students who are passionate. They want students who have real interests and go out of their way to pursue their interests. Choosing to pursue an NTA shows passion because it demonstrates that you are pursuing an interest because the topic itself is intriguing to you, not just because your friends are doing it. If you are engaged in an activity in which teenagers don't typically engage, you are someone who will bring a new point of view to a college classroom and a person who will inspire others to follow their dreams and interests. Colleges love this more than anything!

Many teenagers feel passionate about their relationship with their peers. They fight to protect time with their friends and for their "right" to hang out and do things with their friends. This kind of passion, although real, gets lost because it isn't an NTA, and it does nothing to help an adult tell you from another teenager. If you break the mold by passionately pursuing an NTA, you will stand out.

Lack of passion was the root of my problem with lacrosse. I looked good on paper, but I simply didn't have the passion in the sport that would allow me to excel. I looked like a passionate lacrosse player, but I wasn't. If you have an NTA that you care about, your passion will show through.

NTA Recap

Unless you're a shoo-in for a college, you should figure out an easy way for the admissions counselor to distinguish you from every other teenager who submits an application. Making this distinction is especially difficult for adults because we have little or no understanding of what goes on inside your head. To us, all teenagers are the same unless we know them personally. So, unless the admissions counselor knows you personally, your best bet is to break the teenager mold by actively engaging in an NTA. The NTA will instantly separate you from all the other teenagers who apply and give you a big, fat, greasy, hairy advantage over all of them. Even a student with a questionable academic history (like me) can stand out with the right NTA.

When people tell you to "stand out," they are talking about an NTA. NTAs make kids stand out—period. If you don't have an NTA, you won't stand out. The rest of the tactics in this book will improve your chances whether you have an NTA or not, but they work a lot better if you do.

Chapter 4

THE ZONE-INCREASE YOUR ODDS WITHOUT DOING ANYTHING

Sometimes students are too lazy to engage in a meaningful NTA, or it is already too late to do so before they apply to college. Even if you are one of these unfortunate souls, there is a way to dramatically increase your chances of getting into a competitive college even with a marginal academic record. The strategy is called "Breaking the Zone."

Understanding the Zone

Describing the Zone is simple: it is the most obvious place that you as a student would look for a college to go to. If you are willing to look outside your Zone, you are much more likely to be noticed.

Most students attend college within a few hours of their home. If you're from Illinois, for instance, you are likely to apply to University of Illinois at Urbana-Champaign, University of Illinois at Chicago, Marquette, Lawrence, Purdue, Notre Dame, and perhaps Northwestern and University of Chicago. Your Zone includes these schools and every other student in your Zone shares the same list. So the colleges in this Zone get a lot of applications from similar-looking students. Adults have a hard enough time telling one teenager from the other. Now they have a huge group of students from the same high schools with the same grades and the same sports. What do they do?

The Geography Zone

The answer is they desperately look for alternatives to this mass of similar-looking people. If a school is in your same Zone, rest assured they are more likely to be interested in someone from outside their Zone. All things being equal, a college in Oklahoma would rather take the student from Alaska than one from its own Zone. The reason is simple: a diverse campus enhances education.

When I applied to colleges, my guidance counselor had a tacit understanding of this principle. My grades were so low that my chances of getting into a competitive college were not good. My counselor didn't recommend a college anywhere near my home because she knew I'd probably have no chance. The closest school I applied to was a ten-hour drive away. I went to a college-prep school on the East coast and I was applying to colleges in Washington state and Oregon. It worked, combining

THE GEOGRAPHY ZONE

my willingness to break out of my Zone with my NTA, and I was accepted to several competitive colleges. I didn't even get waitlisted. I didn't have a chance of getting accepted to any school within my Zone, so I had to apply outside my Zone.

Some colleges are so desperate to find students outside their Zone that they will waive your application fee and set you up with a cushy scholarship. Breaking the Zone is one of the best ways to improve your odds of getting accepted.

Different Zones

Geography[25] is probably the biggest Zone and the easiest to understand, but it isn't the only Zone. A Zone is something that is common or expected. Breaking the Zone is uncommon or unexpected. If you are an African American, an HBCU (Historically Black Colleges and Universities) expects you to apply. So, you might be breaking out of the Zone if you apply to a college that *isn't* an HBCU, since most colleges are eager to increase their ethnic diversity. Similarly, if you are not African American and you apply to an HBCU, you will intrigue them. There is also a religious Zone. If you are Jewish, you might be breaking the Zone by applying to a Catholic college. Catholic colleges *expect* Catholic kids to apply, but a Jewish applicant would give them more diversity.

There is a gender Zone too. If you are a male applying to a predominantly female college,[26] your chances go up. Likewise, a female applying to a predominantly male college has a similar experience. The same goes for majors. Colleges love finding

---

25. The geography Zone may not apply to some state schools that have pressure from their state government to attract in-state students.

26. If the college is women-only, men generally don't get accepted; nice try, though.

women who want to study engineering or men who want to study nursing. The major Zone[27] can be used to your advantage in a different way too. In most cases, just because you express interest in a major when you apply doesn't mean you have to stick with a major once you get in. You'll reap the benefit of breaking your Zone and still get to choose what you want. (I, personally, was a pre-med major until I got a terrible grade in chemistry.)[28]

Another, less obvious Zone is the feeder-school Zone. My wife's high school always had a lot of kids who wanted to go to the University of Colorado for college. When a high school sends a lot of their kids to a particular college, they are called "feeder schools" for that college. These relationships are built up over a number of years either because the guidance counselors and the admissions deans have become buddies or because the students from one area tend to have an affinity for the college (they may like skiing, for example). Feeder schools are great for colleges and they do shift a little power to guidance counselors. However, you will be competing with other students from your high school, so it will be even harder to stand out. It's a Zone, and if you are a marginal student, you need to break it. If you are a marginal student, you will have better chances if you avoid applying to a competitive college inside your Zone.

Why Breaking the Zone Works

All colleges want to increase diversity on their campuses. They believe, for good reason, that increased diversity will enrich the

---

27. I always advise kids that if they don't know what they want to major in, then pick the major that will help you get the highest-paying career. Later, when you decide what you do want to major in, I guarantee you won't be upset you went after a lucrative option.

28. Chemistry was an important class for me and this book—more on this later.

educational experience for their students. The Zone leverages the college's natural tendency toward diversity. If you can show that you bring diversity to their campus, they will want you.

If you are clever enough to contact the admissions department before you apply, you can hit them with a line of questioning that will help you uncover the various Zones from which they draw students. Then, you can break the Zone on your application and stand out. The primary Zones you will want to define include geographic, ethnic, academic, athletic, extracurricular, and socio-economic. If you fall outside any of these Zones, you will be a more attractive candidate. If you fall within any of these Zones, you will have to rely more heavily on other tactics (such as your NTA) to make the difference.

When you speak with the admissions staff, you will want to ask questions that will help you understand where you stand. You can be fairly direct. Keep in mind, however, that the college will always want to present itself in the best light, so you may have to dig deeper to uncover the facts. Here is what a typical conversation might sound like with regard to defining Zones.

Mike:	Hi, my name is Mike Moyer. I'm really interested in learning more about State U, and I have a few questions.	*Always tell them who you are. Colleges track these interactions.*
Counselor:	Hi Mike, I'd be happy to answer any questions you might have.	*The counselor may ask you a few questions so they can keep a record of your call.*

Mike:	Great! I'm trying to get a feel for the typical State U student in terms of where they are from and what they study.	*Immediately sets up the conversation to discuss geographic and academic Zones.*
Counselor:	Well, we are very diverse; we have students from all fifty states and over 110 countries. The most popular majors are Engineering and Pharmacy. They are also the most competitive. We were founded as a math and science college, so these kinds of majors tend to be the most competitive.	*Counselors put their best foot forward—he stressed that the campus is very diverse. He also said that the popular majors are the most competitive. If you want information to increase your odds, you will need to figure out what is the least competitive.*
Mike:	Wow, that's great. What is the geographic distribution? Is it pretty even?	*You'll need to clarify the "fifty states" comment. Just about every college can make this claim.*
Counselor:	Well, most of our students come from State. We also draw a lot from Neighbor State One and Neighbor State Two.	*This is typical. Most colleges draw from their local geographies—especially state colleges.*
Mike:	What are the least represented states?	*Further clarification will give you some of the sweet spots for diversity.* (continued)

Counselor:	We don't have many students from the Southeast. In fact, only 3 percent of our student body is from that area.	*Bingo. If you are from the Southeast, you are in great shape. If not, you'll have to break a different Zone or pick a different college.*
Mike:	You mentioned that your popular majors are Engineering and Pharmacy. What are your least popular or what departments are you trying to grow?	*Now dig a little deeper in the academic areas.*
Counselor:	Our fine arts program is excellent, but one of our smaller programs. We are also trying to grow our East Asian Studies department.	*Ah-ha! Another gem. If you are from the Southeast and apply as an East Asian Studies major, you will be more attractive to this college.*

As this over-simplified, but not too unrealistic, conversation shows, asking a few questions can really uncover opportunity. Intuitively, all other things being equal, an East Asian Studies major from the Southeast will have a better chance of getting into this college than an Engineering major from State. After reading viewbooks or websites, many colleges seem more diverse than they really are. They aren't trying to deceive you; they are just putting their best foot forward. Getting students from all fifty states is great, but it doesn't tell the whole picture.

You can learn more about the Zones by talking to an admissions counselor directly than any other method. Colleges may post data about their classes on their websites, but they may not tell the complete picture. Admissions counselors want to help. They want you to know where they need students. (Increasing diversity is *by far* the most popular way colleges use Cappex.) Probing them about unpopular majors will not only give you some good admissions ideas, but also it may introduce you to some very cool majors. East Asian Studies may be your calling!

Knowing the Zones gives you a huge edge. Once you define how you're going to break out of the mold, ask your counselor to drop a note to the admissions department that explains why you aren't the typical student. You will want to highlight your differences in your personal statement, so be sure to ask your guidance counselor or references to direct the admissions staff to your statement.

CARROT:

For a list of additional Zone-defining and Zone-breaking questions, visit CollegePeas.com and enter the word ZONE in the CARROT Box.

Colleges Outside Your Zone

Students often get their heart set on a college that is inside their Zone. This is okay and you can go ahead and apply, but unless you have all your other ducks in a row or are particularly strong academically, be prepared for disappointment. Picking a college outside your Zone does not mean you are compromising. All other things being equal, your chances of being accepted to a college outside your Zone are better than to the one inside the Zone.

If you do have a Zone college in mind, picking a college outside your Zone is easy. Simply pick a college that has the same characteristics you want as the college in your Zone. If the characteristic is "my dad went there" or "the name Harvard," you may be out of luck, but if the characteristic is "small, intimate atmosphere with a solid pre-med program," you are in luck. There are lots of great colleges with similar characteristics.

Figure out what it was about the college in your Zone that you liked and start looking online or ask your guidance counselor for recommendations of similar colleges outside your Zone. Say, "I need a college like X that is outside my Zone." If your counselor is confused, buy them a copy of this book.

Life Outside Your Zone

Stepping out of the Zone makes most people nervous. They picture themselves with no friends in a distant land of strange customs. This is exactly right—for about five minutes.

When you go to college outside your Zone, you will be entering someone else's Zone. By definition, most people at that college will be from within the Zone. You will feel awkward for several reasons. One, you are in a strange land with no friends. This is a problem that is easy to solve with a smile and a handshake. Even nerds make friends fast in college. Nobody wants to keep you out.

In college, the more the merrier is usually true. Second, many of the other people there may be academically more qualified than you. After all, the college may have lowered their academic standards because you were something they wanted. But remember that the college knows that you will add much to the academic environment, and because of that you will flourish academically.

You will probably find that being outside the Zone also has some unexpected perks. Aside from the fact that it gave you an admissions edge over your more academically qualified in-Zone counterparts, you may find that the college has a special place in its institutional heart for people from your Zone. Did you know, for instance, that Creighton University in Omaha, Nebraska, loves students from Hawaii? It's true! They call Omaha the "Maui of the Midwest" and go out of their way to attract Hawaiian students. You can't be much further from the Zone than that. Creighton likes the personality and attitude that Hawaiian students bring with them and they really enjoy the annual luau put on each year by their more than two hundred enrolled students from the Islands. Creighton knows that when students from within their Zone[29] show up on campus and start finding students from Hawaii in their classes, they will have a better educational experience.

They might also call their friends and family and say, "Hey, there's some kid from Hawaii in my class!"

And their parents will say, "Wow! Really? Hawaii? Do they surf?"

And the kid will say, "Yeah, but he was sick of the beach and wanted to try something new. Can you believe he was actually *tired* of the *beach* in Hawaii?"

And the parents will say, "I can't believe it! I've got to meet this kid. Invite him for Thanksgiving!" So, not only will the

---

29. Creighton's Zone includes good students from Nebraska, Iowa, Missouri, and Kansas.

Hawaiian kid make class more interesting, but he will also make lots of new friends.

Being from outside the Zone is a pretty nice place to be. I had the same experience being from the East coast and going to Kansas for college. I had a number of invitations for Thanksgiving every year I was there. Being from outside the Zone gave me a little cache that went a long way.

Being from outside the Zone may make you nervous and it can be scary, but it will only last a few minutes. In fact, the reason it works so well is because so many students can't get over that fear, so they choose a college within their Zone. Your willingness to step outside the Zone will pay off.

Chapter 5

THE NERVE-BE WHAT THEY WANT TO BE

In my many discussions with admissions deans, I find that the best ones have a qualitative definition of what their school is all about. This element represents something they value, and I call it the "Nerve." If the college sees how you fit into their Nerve, your chances of being accepted will be greater. So, while you are encouraged to break the Zone, you are also encouraged to strike the Nerve.

Nerves are different than Zones. Zones help you leverage a college's tendency toward *diversity* while a Nerve can help you leverage a college's tendency toward *unity*. Basically, colleges want a diverse student body that will all love the same thing: college. A Nerve is the common bond among the students that makes the place special and interesting. It's the common ground that allows a diverse population to bond.

Scott Friedhoff, the Vice President for Enrollment at Allegheny College in Meadville, Pennsylvania, likes students who have combinations of interests that he affectionately calls the "wonderfully weird." For instance, a person with a wonderfully weird combination of interests might be someone who wants to have a double major in biology and music. To the admissions office of Allegheny College, students like this will help create a very interesting and diverse student body and fit the culture of the college.

"Wonderfully weird" is Allegheny's Nerve. If you can demonstrate that you have a wonderfully weird combination of interests, then Allegheny will get excited about your potential as a student. In effect, they are telling you the secret of finding the way to their heart.

You'll have to really pay attention to uncover the Nerve of the school you're interested in. Allegheny likes to use the phrase "wonderfully weird," but they specifically refer to the combinations of academic interests you may have (not general weirdness). These subtleties are important. You don't want to "sum up" a college in a way they might not like. If you told Allegheny that you yourself are weird, you may get a cool reception.

Lawrence University in Appleton, Wisconsin, has a Nerve that may sound similar to Allegheny's, but it is not the same. Steve Syverson, Vice President for Enrollment at Lawrence, characterizes their students as "individualized learners," "multi-interested," and "community engaged." This reflects the fact that students at Lawrence also have uncommon combinations of interests. While this may sound a little like "wonderfully weird" at Allegheny, both colleges understand themselves as unique; you must embrace these nuances and use them to your advantage. For instance, if you are applying to Lawrence and you have no idea what you want to study, just tell them you are "multi-interested" as opposed to "undecided"…it will be music to their ears!

While most colleges have a Nerve, they are not all as well-defined as Allegheny's and Lawrence's. In fact, some colleges have a really hard time identifying their Nerve and are even less adept at communicating it. Rest assured, however, that there is a Nerve.

Striking the Nerve

Striking the Nerve requires you to do a little detective work into the messages that the college sends. I know one college in Colorado that likes to find students interested in the great outdoors. In fact, the first few words on their website are "Surrounded by stunning mountains…" They actively promote their outdoor adventures program, and they have pictures of the scenery on their brochures. This college knows that if you love the outdoors, you will love their college.

Colleges don't mind taking academic risks on students who hit their Nerve because those students are more likely to be happy and content on their campus. And, if they are happy and content, they are more likely to do well, graduate, and become great alums.

To find a college's Nerve, you can start by visiting their website and flipping through their viewbook. You may find lots of pictures of musicians or people on boats. So, if you can demonstrate your love of music or love of the sea, you will be striking the Nerve. It doesn't even matter if you can play an instrument or if you don't know how to swim. Your love and appreciation for something the college takes seriously will help you stand apart.

Once you identify the college's Nerve, you will have to relate to it through your essays, interviews, and other interactions with the college. Even your choice of who provides you with references can help you strike the Nerve. If you were applying to Allegheny, for instance, you might pick an eclectic teacher over the more straight-laced choice.

Striking the Nerve is showing that you are what they want you to be. It's about showing that you are compatible with their campus and their values. If the college's Nerve has to do with their focus on the environment, be sure to use recycled paper for all your correspondence. If their Nerve is related to their heritage, you might write an essay that includes a historical perspective.

Understanding Nerves

Colleges can have all kinds of different Nerves. Sometimes they are obvious. For example, George Washington University in Washington, DC, is likely to value someone who values politics. If the Nerve is not obvious, you'll have to do some research to figure out what the common elements are at the college. Some popular places to look for the Nerve are:

- **Political orientation.** Is the college liberal or conservative?
- **Art.** Do they promote art and culture on their campus?
- **Sports.** Do they value supportive fans?
- **Local culture.** Does the college identify with the local culture?
- **Heritage.** Does the college identify with certain roots? (Are they Irish?)

- **Environment.** How important is the physical environment around the college? Are they looking for urban types or those who like the country?
- **Founders.** What did they have in mind when they started the college?
- **Local business.** Who supports the college by hiring its graduates and donating money?
- **Original charter.** What need was the college created to fill?

Appealing to a college's Nerve assures them that you will have a bond with the other students on their campus. It is what allows a very diverse group of individuals to live in harmony. It is the common ground for uncommon people. Remember, Zones help you leverage a college's tendency toward *diversity* while a Nerve can help you leverage a college's tendency toward *unity*. Nothing is sweeter on a college campus than a group of different people who all love being students at the same college.

Take a look back at the last chapter's sample conversation with the admissions counselor at State U. The counselor mentioned that Engineering and Pharmacy are popular majors because they have a focus on math and science. East Asian Studies may not be popular because of the college's math and science focus. The counselor said the college was founded as a math and science college, and they probably pride themselves on the technical aspects of education. To them, art means architecture and writing means technical specs. Clearly the Nerve of the college is left-brained. So, you can give yourself an additional edge if you develop a passion for early East Asian Studies as it pertains to the math and science of East Asia vs. the art, history, and literature. If your interest is genuine, you will accomplish two things that will increase your chances of getting in: first, you will break the Zone (by choosing an underrepresented major), and second, you will strike the Nerve (by having a passion for math and science). Couple this with a good NTA and you have become the college's dream student—even if your grades are marginal.

Be careful not to confuse a Nerve and a Zone—the mistake can be devastating. Nerves are core elements of how the college identifies and differentiates itself. If you were applying to State U and treated the math and science element like a Zone to break, the college would seriously question why you were applying if you weren't interested in math and science.

I mentioned earlier that applying to an HBCU if you're not black might be a good Zone to break. However, many HBCUs consider their HBCU status a core element of their education. In this case having a predominately African American student body is part of their Nerve, not their Zone.

There is another benefit to striking the Nerve of a college that is more important than getting in—you will have a better overall college experience. Students whose interests and style strike the Nerve of a college will have found a college that is a good fit, and as I said earlier, nothing is more important than fit.

College Fit and the Nerve

One of the great things about finding the college's Nerve is that it will help you assess your potential fit with that college. Because nothing is more important than fit, if you can see yourself as someone who strikes the Nerve of the college, you will probably feel right at home there. I liked art and science—a wonderfully weird combination of interests. Who knows? I might have been right at home at Allegheny or Lawrence.

CARROT:

For a list of additional examples of the Nerve, visit CollegePeas.com and enter the word NERVE in the CARROT Box.

Chapter 6

YOUR APPLICATION TEAM— MAKING IT WORK FOR YOU

Good college applications are not completed by individuals; they are completed by teams. At the core of the team are you (the captain), your high school counselor, high school administrative assistants, your references, your parents, and even the admissions counselor who may be putting together some paperwork on your behalf. Don't ignore these people. They are *not* paper-pushers, they are part of your team, and if you work with them properly, they will be an extremely valuable part of your success. The mere fact that you treat them as a team will impress them. Most people treat them like assistants and never even say thank you (do not forget to send thank-you notes).[30]

The nice thing about your team is that they can contact the admissions department and talk you up so you won't have to brag about yourself in person. This adds much to your credibility.

---

30. Thank-you notes are key, especially if you have to go back to your references for a second round of applications.

When someone speaks on your behalf, you gain mucho credibility. To be a good team leader, you will have to carefully pick your team and make sure you give them enough time to prepare and execute what you will need from them. Early is better than late. Many colleges having rolling admissions, which can mean that the sooner you get your application in, the sooner you will be accepted. Most colleges receive a stack of FedEx envelopes on the application deadline date. Waiting to the last minute will rarely improve your odds.

Starting Early–Really Early

If you are reading this book during your freshman or sophomore year of high school, you are in luck. The college application can be a powerful planning tool that will show you exactly what you need to do to get accepted to a competitive college. Here's how it works.

Pick out a college that looks interesting to you. It doesn't really matter which college you choose because your mind is bound to change. Just make sure it's competitive.

Complete the application as accurately as you can with your current credentials. You will have to leave a lot of holes (like test scores, for instance).

Pretend you are a senior and fill the application out again. You will have to complete the application using the credentials you think you will need to get accepted. What will your grades have to be? What will your test scores need to be? Will you have an NTA? Is the college you chose outside your Zone?

Congratulations! You now have a complete roadmap for success! Your job over the next few years is to move from where you

YOUR APPLICATION TEAM

are today to where you want to be based on what your future application looks like. Knowing where you are going is the first step in getting there. Most freshmen and sophomores haven't even thought about how they are going to get into college. In fact, most juniors and seniors don't either. This application exercise will only take a few hours, but they will be some of the most important hours in your college planning process.

If you are reading this as a junior or senior, this can be a good exercise anyway. Familiarizing yourself with the actual application will help you think about the information you need and get you more comfortable with the process. You can download as many applications as you want free of charge, so there is no downside to getting a stack and looking through them. The application itself can give you insight into the Nerve of the college, especially the essay questions. Many colleges like to ask students to write essay questions that help them assess the students' fit with their college.

CARROT:

To download a typical college application, visit CollegePeas.com and enter the word APPLICATION in the CARROT Box.

The Application

The application for the college you choose is pretty much like every other college's application. In fact, applications are so similar from college to college that there is such a thing as the Common Application or the Universal College Application that allows you to complete just one application for many colleges. You just click to apply. It's so easy that kids click to apply, click to apply, click to apply so much that they drive their teachers and high school counselors crazy. Every time *you* apply, *they* have to jump through hoops sending out recommendations and transcripts. Pick a few colleges that are good matches, apply the rules in this book, and you'll be fine—you won't need to hedge your bets by applying to a million colleges. There are a lot of students who apply to five, ten, or more colleges (twenty-eight is the highest number I've heard of). It causes a lot of "chatter" among guidance counselors who don't appreciate all the extra work. There are two situations where applying to a high number makes sense. The first is if you have very specialized interests like steel-drum design and building where you may want to apply to every college that offers those programs. The second is if you have high financial needs and need a "full ride." No matter what the case, have a heart-to-heart conversation with your guidance counselor before submitting more than five to ten applications.

What's important to understand about the application is that although it is designed to collect information they want to know, it is much more about giving them information you want them to know.

By the way, no matter what anyone tells you, *assume* that a human being will never read your application and that a computer will do the first cut. There is a good chance that it actually will be read, but this book is about beating the odds. You want to make sure it is read. So, unless you are clearly in the 100-percent in category, you should take some steps to ensure your application is given the attention it deserves. Smaller liberal arts colleges tend to spend more time with an application than a larger public college, but if you still assume that no human will read your application, you will be on the safe side. It's your job to make sure they read it. This is where your team can help.

References

The people who will provide your references (aka recommendations) are important members of your team, but they are much more than just form completers. The reference form is often a formality that shows the college that you are able to jump through a few hoops. Colleges generally *expect* your references to be positive. So they can be a less important part of the package. However, if you have a bad reference, then it will probably hurt you more than you might expect. A bad reference shows 1) that you may not be a good prospect and 2) that you suck at choosing references. Colleges want students who show good judgment.

Using the team concept, however, you can think of the reference form as a datasheet that outlines your relationship with the reference. So, when your reference calls the office on your behalf and refers them to your essays, the admissions counselor doesn't have to scratch his or her head thinking, "Who the heck was that?" They can simply glance at your reference forms to see that the person calling was the former president of the alumni association and a member of the board of directors of the charity you started to relocate pesky raccoons.

If your academic record is weak, you may have been relegated to the out basket pretty quick. In this case, you'll have to find a way to make sure you are being considered. One way is to invite each of your references to contact the admissions office or some other influential person (like a tenured professor or powerful alumnus) on your behalf in addition to submitting the reference form. This can be a personal call, an e-mail, a handwritten note, or an in-person visit. Discuss the contact before it's made and coach the reference on what to say.

Good references will make contact on your behalf. Usually, your guidance counselor is one of your references, and they are already engaged in the process. They will do whatever it takes to make sure you get the best shot at getting in. However, if you need references to contact the college and you have a reference who isn't willing to contact the college, you should consider finding another reference who will. Even if you already submitted your reference quota, you can still pick a new person, ask them to complete a reference form for you and then ask them to make a contact on your behalf. Your file will have an extra reference in it, but the college may not notice or may not care. Even if they don't like it, you are probably going to offset any negative impact with the positive impact of having a good advocate in your file.

It is not uncommon for a reference to be hesitant to make contact on your behalf. This is usually because you chose a teacher or coach who serves as a reference for a lot of people and aren't used to going out on a limb. Many colleges recommend that you provide references from teachers. However, only ask a teacher if they would be a good member of your team. If you weren't a star student, you may have trouble finding a teacher who will contact a college on your behalf and keep a straight face. I remember thinking that I was going to be a doctor when I grew up, so I asked my biology teacher to provide a reference. She rescued me from my stupidity by telling me that she would have trouble recommending me because of my poor performance in her class (she wasn't really even that nice about it). I can thank her now. If she had said yes, I would have had a bad reference (ouch). I wound up asking my French teacher instead. Although I had only slightly better grades in French, I also helped him organize a trip to Quebec, which scored me a few brownie points. Still not a great reference, but better than a reference who didn't even like me in the first place.

This is a problem that all non-star students face. So, unless a college specifically *requires* that your reference is a teacher, do not feel obligated to provide a teacher reference. Pick the people you think will do the best job representing you to a college whether they are teachers or not. A reference is a member of your team; choose them wisely.

If you have an NTA, you should have plenty of adults who will be willing to serve on your team as references. Don't worry about making sure you have teachers and coaches. Conventional wisdom dictates that you choose someone who knows you well. This really isn't important. You are picking and choosing your team. Pick and choose the people who are willing to help you get in, not the people who are just going to fill out a form on your behalf.

BONUS CHAPTER!

To read the bonus chapter about finding references, visit CollegePeas.com and enter the word STRANGER in the CARROT Box.

Coaching Your References

It's smart to prep your references in advance of any contact they make on your behalf. Make sure they know a few things about you, especially your NTA and how you are breaking your Zone. If you have anything in particular that you think might be a problem (like your grades or test scores), make sure they know about them. Also, unless they know someone personally that they can call, you will have to give them the name and number of a good contact. If you know which admissions counselor is handling your application, this is a good contact person.[31] A good contact from a reference would sound something like this.

Reference:	Hi, my name is Mike Moyer, and I'm calling on behalf of Millie Foley. I'm one of her references.	*Your reference identifies himself and why he is calling.*
Counselor:	Hello Mr. Moyer, how may I help you?	*The counselor will be confused; most references don't call.*

---

31. Small schools often assign a specific admissions counselor to your application. For me it was the guy who handled anyone whose last name began with M.

Reference:	I just wanted to make sure I spoke to someone personally to emphasize my support for Millie's application. I was on the board of directors for a charity that Millie started last year that helped refurbish old computers to give to underprivileged families.	*Hits hard with the NTA.*
Counselor:	Really? What was the student's name again?	*Counselor is immediately impressed—how did he miss this one? The grades and test scores may have been so low that he ignored the rest.*
Reference:	Millie Foley.	*He is searching for the application.*
Counselor:	Hmm, Foley. Let me see if I have her file. Oh yes, here it is.	*He is taking it out of the trash and dusting off the pencil shavings.*
Reference:	You have her application there? Millie from New York?	*Establishes the geographic Zone.*

Counselor:	Yes, I have it here. I see that you are the president of CollegePeas.com! We love that site!	*Counselor has found the reference form so he knows who he is talking to.*
Reference:	Thank you very much, how nice of you to say. I hope you will take some extra time to read Millie's essay about her charity; it's very impressive. Also, she is really looking forward to the chance to study in such a great, historic city next year. I know her grades aren't on par with a typical student of yours, but she really is a passionate and hard-working kid. She wrote a great essay. Have you had a chance to read it?	*Addressed the poor grades, struck the Nerve, and re-emphasized the NTA. He also has been put on the spot with regard to the essays.*
Counselor:	I haven't had a chance to read it yet, but I will make sure I do. She does sound impressive. I will make sure I take another look at her application.	*Millie is back on the "Maybe" pile, soon to be on the "In" pile.*

After a while the counselor will have received numerous contacts from various people bragging about how great Millie is. This is highly unusual, especially for a kid with low grades. Millie must be a diamond in the rough. She will be admitted.

It is important to note that if you apply to too many schools, your references will grow weary of making these calls. They may be happy to make one or two, but making ten or twenty calls will make you look like a scatterbrain. Limit the number of colleges you apply to. Applying to too many colleges hurts everyone.

Stuffing the Ballot Box

I managed a band[32] in college called Mountain Clyde that competed in a contest at a local bar in Lawrence, Kansas, called the Bottleneck. The contest was to decide which band the bar would sponsor to attend the South by Southwest (SXSW) music conference in Austin, Texas. The conference was a big deal. There were lots of record companies floating around town and it was not unusual for bands to get "discovered" at SXSW.

On the night Mountain Clyde played, the Bottleneck was packed. We asked every one of our friends and relatives to come out and vote for us. We won. All the other bands were angry because they didn't think that Mountain Clyde was the best band and that all we did was have our friends stuff the ballot box. That is exactly what we did. We stuffed the ballot box because we really wanted to go to SXSW.

The managers of the Bottleneck weren't born yesterday. They're not music critics. They held the competition to sell beers. They were happy to give us the door receipts for the trip to Austin.

---

32. Bands, in general, aren't good NTAs unless you get a professional record deal.

Not only did we help them sell beer, but they also knew we really wanted to go. The other bands, however talented, didn't show nearly as much interest as we did. It wasn't about who was the best,[33] *it was about who showed the most interest.*

When your references and guidance counselor contact the college on your behalf, they are essentially stuffing the ballot box for you. Every time you or someone else makes positive contact with the school on your behalf, a "vote" is being cast in your favor. They can vote for you over and over. And guess what—colleges keep track! They call this "expressed interest," and it helps them pick the students who are most likely to say yes if they are offered admission to their college. These students are great because colleges make a safe bet if they extend them an offer. Colleges *love* students who are interested in them because they really love students who enroll.

You can stuff the ballot box in your favor by making lots of positive contact with the colleges. Variety is important too. Calling them one hundred times a day isn't going to work. If you harass the admissions counselor, this tactic will backfire and you will damage your chances of getting in. In order to cast a vote for yourself, you need to meet the admissions counselors at college fairs, during online chat sessions,[34] at alumni networking events, or at anything else that a college does to reach out. Fill out the business reply card on every piece of mail the college sends you, go to the college's information session at your high school, and send an instant message to the admissions counselor to tell him or her good news about your chemistry test. Handwritten thank-you

---

33. Mountain Clyde got a Capitol Records contract based on contacts they made at SXSW.

34. Online chats are great! Colleges are trying to make chats work, but few students actually participate. If you actually participate, you will get noticed.

notes to everyone that you meet related to the college are among the best ways to stuff the ballot box. Keep showing interest and you will stuff the ballot box.

CARROT:

For more ideas on stuffing the ballot box, visit CollegePeas.com and enter the word BALLOT in the CARROT Box.

Financial Information

You will also be asked to complete some financial data. Most colleges will say they are "need blind," but I was leery about completing this because I didn't want a college to think that I wasn't ready to pay in full for my education. This is a hunch, but as far as I can tell, there is little downside to waiting until after you get accepted to complete the financial aid section unless you aren't paying attention and miss the financial aid deadline. If you do miss the deadline, you can still get loans, but you might have some trouble getting free cash like scholarships and grants. On the upside, you can save yourself a little time.

Essays and Personal Statements

College essay questions often include the option to pick your own topic or write a personal statement. This is where you will highlight your NTA and address why you are outside their Zone. If the application does not include the option to pick your own topic or write a personal statement, you can submit one anyway (in addition to the required essays). Not all colleges appreciate this kind of extra material, but if the message is important, you can overcome any negative impact the additional material has. You can always include information about your NTA in your cover letter.

The college essay is notorious for how often it is written by people other than the actual college applicant. This is bad—really bad. Write it yourself, run it through spell check, and make sure the topic is about your NTA. Be sure to ask someone to read your essay and edit it for grammar but not style—colleges *crave* authenticity and if they even suspect that you paid a service to write your essay, it will leave a very bad impression. I even heard about counselors who advise a few strategic spelling or grammar errors just to make the essay look less "professional."

When it comes to the essay, it's all about the story. If you have something good to write it won't matter if you're not Shakespeare.[35] If you don't have something good to write about, then it doesn't matter how well it's written.

Most colleges claim they read every essay that comes in. However, if your grades are sketchy, they may not give your essay the attention it deserves. If you are worried about this, ask a member of your team to contact the admissions counselor who is handling your file. Your team member can reiterate their support for your admission and ask the admissions counselor to make sure they pay special attention to your optional essay—the one about how you started a clinic in Africa to help AIDS victims. An e-mail or voicemail will suffice—you never want to be too pushy. The admissions counselor will not forget you or your essay, and

---

35. This doesn't mean it can suck, it just means you don't have to kill yourself making it perfect.

they will become a member of your team. You can leverage this relationship during your interview.

By the way, I've mentioned several times that the college admissions counselor is also a member of your team. If you are going to get out of the Maybe stack, you will need an advocate on the inside who will argue your case in front of the admissions committee. If you build a personal relationship with the admissions counselor by keeping in touch, making sure they have a complete application and being respectful, you will make them a member of your team.

Interviews

Unless you are a shoo-in, don't skip the interview. This is where you will load up the admissions counselor with powerful pneumonic devices with which to remember you. Remember, I brought a homing pigeon with me to the interview and asked the interviewer to write a note that I promptly attached to the bird and let it go. I called the admissions counselor later and read her note back to her. It's hard to forget that little experience.

Interviews often happen before you apply, but rest assured that they will impact your chances of getting in. Use this time to highlight the important NTA you have been doing. Also, make sure you bring attention to how you break the Zone. This is a good time to ask some Zone-defining and Zone-breaking questions so you can make sure you are properly breaking out of the mold (most kids try to fit the mold). Likewise, an in-person interview can help you identify the Nerve and determine whether the college is a good fit.

Sending Stuff

If you have provided what the college asked for in your application, you have done only half your job. Make sure you insert newspaper clippings that cover the impact your NTA had on the community.[36] Include pictures of the product you made or copies of the materials you developed for your charity. Make sure the stuff is tangible. If you made a movie, send the review in addition to a DVD (but don't expect the DVD to be watched; only coaches watch videos).

Sending stuff does not mean you have to assemble a "me portfolio" filled with all sorts of random things that "make you you." Portfolios about you are a big, fat waste of time and make you look like a dork. Send *only* items that will highlight your NTA. If your samples are big, send pictures. Don't send anything perishable, like baked goods.

Unless you are applying for a web development major, do not send a link to an online portfolio unless they specifically ask for one. It is a waste of time and will probably not get viewed. Even the biggest college admissions department still maintains paper files on their applicants. When they are sitting in a committee meeting to review applications, they are not, I repeat, *not* looking at your online portfolio. Personal web pages, social networking sites, or online portfolios *hurt* applications more often than they help. Colleges use college application files to make decisions. They do not use personal websites or social networking profiles. I have never heard a case where this kind of material has helped a student get in (but I have heard of cases where it hurts).

This is not about bribes. Do not include gifts, cash, or gag gifts.

---

36. Getting press coverage for your NTA is easy; just call a few local papers and tell them what you are up to. They will be impressed.

These items are for desperate losers. I once heard of a guy sending a stuffed sock with a note saying, "I just wanted to get my foot in the door!"[37] Ouch! What a dork! The key part about sending stuff is to only send things that can make your NTA more concrete and stand out.

A college application is a stack of paper (or at least electronic paper) that a college uses to organize information about applicants. The application itself is not the end game; it is simply part of the process that will get you in. Most students mail in their application or click "submit" and then wash their hands of it while they wait for a response. The successful applicant engages their application team and makes sure that no stone is left unturned. Applications, in themselves, can only do so much. Leverage your team if you truly want the edge.

---

37. This particular tactic is not uncommon and it makes an admissions counselor cringe and feel embarrassed for you.

Chapter 7

LIFE IS FULL OF SECOND CHANCES–TAKING YOUR MULLIGAN

So what happens if you engage in a stellar NTA, break the Zone, strike the Nerve, and rally a world-class application team and you still get a skimpy little rejection letter from the college you thought would welcome you with open arms? As painful as this will be, it happens and it's not the end of the world (I promise). Hopefully you applied to several colleges and at least one accepted you. However, if you did your very best and still got rejected, it doesn't mean that you can't still get into a competitive college. You have a number of second chances.

Appeals

Some colleges actually have a formal appeals process you can go through if you don't get accepted the first time you apply. The process usually includes a personal interview during which the college will assess your interest and review your application to make sure they didn't make a mistake. College admissions counselors are at least part human and they do, on occasion, make mistakes. Their appeals process will allow a rejected student to get another chance.

If you did the right thing at the college that rejected you and made a connection with the admissions counselor, then you have their phone number. Call them[38] and ask them if they can help you understand why you weren't accepted. Explain to them that you had your heart set on their college and you are really disappointed, and that any information they provide will be helpful. Don't feel bad if they can't give you a straight answer; it may be against the college's policy or they may not actually know why you were rejected. In many cases they simply ran out of room before they could take you out of the Maybes.

Also ask them about the policy on reapplying, and if the college has an appeals process. You may have to wait, but you might be able to reapply to some alternative programs. Ask what you can do to get another chance and if they can suggest anything that will improve your chances. Do you need to attend summer school? Try to get the admissions counselor on your side.

If a college does not have a formal appeals process, they probably have at least an informal appeals process. They will often review your file and tell you what you will need to do in order

---

38. Don't call if you are upset. Wait a few days until you cool down. You should be upbeat and positive. You are eager to give it another try.

to get accepted. This could include something as simple as getting a certain GPA during your final semester in high school. Sometimes the college will recommend a few semesters at a community college.

Colleges are very interested in students who push for an appeal because it shows great interest in the college. Colleges love students who are really passionate about attending. If they are keeping you out, it is probably because they found a few skeletons in your closet or they are afraid you won't be able to handle the work. You will need to figure out a way to improve your grades. We'll talk more about this later.

It's Not Too Late to Pick Another College

If you don't find out that you got rejected until May, you can still apply somewhere else, even if people tell you the application deadline has passed. Many competitive colleges have rolling admission and don't have deadlines. Others will overlook your late application if you are a student they really want. It is quite possible that applying late could work in your favor. The college may have empty spots that they really need to fill. Even competitive colleges can have empty spots. This doesn't mean deadlines aren't important—they are. If you "blow off" a deadline, you will damage your credibility. But if you are serious about getting a second chance, you will have to apply in spite of the deadlines.

Backdoor Admissions-Alternative Programs

Whether you reapply or want to apply to a different competitive school, you should consider alternative programs.

The first thing you need to keep in mind is that the program you applied to may have been the *most* competitive of all the programs that college offers. Let's say you are a high school senior. You probably applied to enter the freshman class to start this fall. Guess what? So did everybody else. The competition for the spots in the full-time undergraduate, on-campus program is probably the highest. Many schools have alternative routes that are less competitive.

I applied to the University of Chicago's Graduate School of Business (the "GSB") several years after I left college. The GSB was, and still is, one of the most competitive programs in the United States. I had some good experience after I graduated from college and I had learned to make good grades, but I wanted to make sure I was in the 100-percent group. So, I applied to the part-time program, and it worked. The GSB offers a full-time program, a weekend program, and a part-time program. Students applying to the full-time program compete with students from all over the world. Students applying to the weekend program compete with students all over the Midwest who are willing to fly or drive in for classes on the weekends. Students who apply to the part-time program compete only with other local students. The competition is much less for the part-time program, although the education is identical (so is the price, unfortunately). Once you're in the alternative, it is usually pretty easy to transfer into the full-time program if you want.

By taking advantage of this backdoor entrance, I secured myself a spot at one of the top business schools in the world. I had other things going for me too, but why take the risk by trying to elbow my way through the front door?

Keep an eye out for these back doors; they come in many forms. When most people think about college, they think "full-time, day classes." But many undergraduate colleges offer part-time, night classes, and even distance learning and online classes. Some colleges will allow you to take classes one at a time. Some will allow you to enroll as a "student-at-large" and take classes without actually being an enrolled degree-seeking student. Ask about these programs when you speak to the admissions departments. These programs are easier to get into and will pave your way into the program you are after. After earning a few decent grades in these alternative programs, you will have little or no problem transferring to a full-time program.

Some colleges have summer programs that translate nicely into full-time enrollment. If you got rejected, try to enroll in summer school instead of waiting until the fall. You may be able to obtain a "conditional admit," which means you're in, but you have to keep your grades up.

Backdoor admissions are a great way to improve your chances of getting in. In a way, it is similar to breaking the Zone. Colleges want people to apply to programs that are less popular.

Forging a New Path

Admissions departments love gutsy moves. It takes guts to walk into the office and make an appointment with the dean of admissions to argue your case. I know a guy who got into Georgetown by forging a new path. It was a college that only offered fall admission. He walked into the admissions office at Georgetown, sat down with the dean of admissions, and proceeded to make his case about why they should admit him as a mid-year student. He was in the next day. Granted, he was a solid student, but he made an exceptional request. The odds were against him in spite of his solid academic record—the university did not offer mid-year enrollment.

This happens more than you might think. In college admissions many things are negotiable and the more you're willing to push them to talk, the more likely they are to be impressed and give you a shot. Forging a new path isn't about being a good student and then sitting around waiting for someone to notice. It is about taking a bold action along untraveled roads.

A bold way to forge a new path with the college is to put forth a challenge. Tell them that you want to attend their college and you are willing to do what it takes to get it. An admissions counselor told me about a woman who wanted in so badly that she mailed her deposit check even after she was rejected. She included a letter that said she was going to enroll in community college and take classes similar to those she would have taken as a freshman at the college. The letter outlined a bet—she would make straight A's at community college for a year in exchange for admission. If she did not get straight A's, the college could keep the deposit check and deny her admission. The dean of admissions mailed back the

check but told the student that if she kept up her side of the bargain, there would be a spot open for her in the sophomore class.

Hail Mary

If the admissions counselor thinks that you barely missed the cut, you can do a Hail Mary. Set up a meeting with the dean of admissions and make your case. Be professional, friendly, and understanding. Don't make excuses, don't cry—just tell your story and let it shine.

At this point, don't be afraid to break some rules. People often think your second application will be ignored if you have already applied once. It won't be ignored if it has a good NTA, it breaks the Zone, it hits the Nerve, and your team is behind you. It also won't be ignored if you hand-deliver it to the dean's office and explain you want a second chance. Don't expect the dean to welcome you. You will probably get a cold reception, or you might even get shown the door. Colleges deal with lots of angry students and parents. Be polite, be respectful, but be persistent. It's easy to dismiss an applicant who barges into the office in a fit of rage. It's harder to ignore a student who has a passionate commitment to proving him or herself to a college. You won't be able to submit the same application; you'll have to write new essays, submit new references, and pay the fee again (don't expect to get a two-for-one deal with the fee). Change as much as you can, but the core information will still be the same. Try again, even if the college tells you not to. At this point you *have nothing to lose*. Go for it!

I met a girl who got accepted to a highly competitive college the *day before* the classes started. She showed up with her application, made a good case, and got accepted. It happens, and it might as well be you. It definitely *won't* happen if you don't give it a try.

There is more to getting into college than meets the eye. The process often blinds us so much that we don't see the alternatives. Admissions isn't an exact science, and there are countless ways for the determined student to get to where they want to be. If the rules and the process aren't getting you where you want, then rewrite the rules. Work with the admissions department, let them know how you feel, and be willing to do what it takes to make the difference.

Chapter 8

LIFE IS FULL OF THIRD CHANCES–GETTING IN WHEN YOU STILL DIDN'T GET IN

I f you took your second chance and got rejected again, you may have an academic problem you need to overcome. One of the cold, hard truths of college admissions is that in spite of your best efforts, the bulk of your admissions advantage comes from your GPA and your test scores. The ideas in this book can't save every student. Colleges have to make sure you can handle the coursework. Even the most interesting student in the world will get turned down if they don't appear to be capable of handling the work.

Competitive colleges, especially highly competitive colleges, often don't have admissions departments—they have *rejection* departments. Many competitive colleges reject more applications than they accept, and it seems they are constantly on the lookout for reasons to reject you. Your grades and test scores are the number one reason you will get rejected. The ideas in this book will do wonders to overcome poor academic performance, but they can't save everyone. Even if you performed as poorly as I did (or worse), there is still hope, and the following strategies can help you turn yourself around.

Until now, all the ideas in this book have been *offensive* moves. They have been designed to make you stand out among your peers, get noticed, and get in. If you are in the 100-percent out category or at the low end of the Maybes, it's not enough to have a good offensive strategy; you must also develop a defensive strategy. If you aren't sure where you stand, try implementing these strategies right away.

Defensive Strategy

A defensive strategy is one that prevents a college admissions department from tossing your application in the shredder *after* they have made a tentative decision to let you in. In other words, you have won them with your offensive strategy, but they just can't bring themselves to accept you when they look at your grades. You must find a way to defend yourself against this kind of event. At the core of your defensive strategy is your grade curve or grade pattern. This is the progress of your overall GPA over time.

The bottom line is that if you want to develop a defensive strategy, you will need to figure out a way to improve your grades. If you are a student with average or poor grade performance, this probably sounds a lot harder than it is. You may be happy to know that improving your grades is not about "buckling down and hitting the books." In fact, you may find, as I did, that getting good grades actually requires *less* work than getting bad grades. You can do it. I promise.

You will need to spend some time at a less-competitive college and then re-apply to your competitive college as a transfer student after you develop a defensive strategy. Remember, there are lots and lots of great non-competitive colleges. When I started attending KU (considered a less-competitive college at the time), I wouldn't have dreamed of transferring out.[39]

Defensive strategies are an important part of getting into a competitive college, but as you will see in the next section, you have to plan ahead.

Grade Stories

Grade stories are an essential part of a good defensive plan. You can still get by on a terrible GPA if you have a good grade story. You have one real shot at a grade story. Here's how it works: First, you have to develop a good grade curve. A grade curve is the line your grades make when you chart them on a graph like the examples later in this section. (Don't actually show anybody the graph itself; just use it to help you plan your story). A good curve starts out at a low point and steadily slants upward. You have to make sure that no matter how low your grades go, they "dip" only once. The dip is the lowest point at which your grade curve stops trending down and starts trending up. If you have more than one dip in your grade curve, it means you brought your grades up one semester and they went down again the next. If you have more than one dip, you really have to do some tap-dancing to make it

---

39. That's not *completely* true. I did consider transferring to Tulane and I did consider join-ing the Army, but those are stories for a different time.

work. Next, you must have at least as many semesters after the dip as before (preferably more). In the semesters after the dip, you must show a steadily improving GPA.

By the way, I'm talking about *cumulative* GPA and not *individual* semester GPA. A student with a bad GPA will never become a 4.0 student. It is mathematically impossible. You can't change your past. If you dip to a 1.7 GPA (as I did), you will probably never pull your total GPA above 3.0. That's okay. Focus on creating an upward trend. I was accepted to a highly competitive graduate school, and my cumulative GPA was a 2.6. It's not so much your final GPA that matters but the most recent trend in your GPA. If your recent GPA trends up, you are in good shape. This means there can be some variance from semester to semester. However, pace yourself. If you do too well too soon, you may not be able to maintain it. For instance, if you take easy classes one semester to raise your GPA, you may get killed the next semester if you wind up tackling some harder classes and don't do as well. If your overall GPA trends down or even if it has more than one dip, you're pretty much toast.

The last part of a grade story is the explanation. You must give an honest, plausible explanation for your poor performance and be able to demonstrate that, after you pulled yourself out of your misfortune, you were able to get your grades on track and that your recent grades more accurately reflect your academic abilities.

I personally had a series of decreasing GPAs followed by a series of improving GPAs until my last semester in college when I got a 4.0. It took me five years to create the right grade curve. The faster you get your grade curve right, the faster you can apply for a transfer. By the time I had mine right I was ready to graduate!

Good Grade Patterns

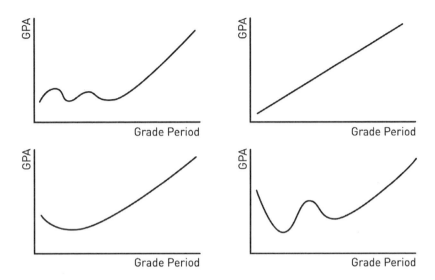

Bad Grade Patterns

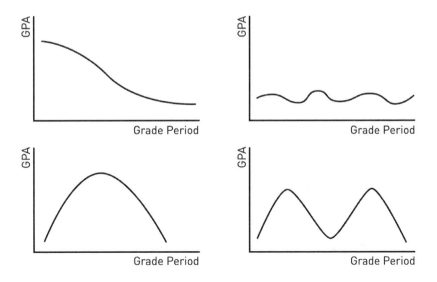

Now that I had my grade curve laid out properly, with steadily increasing grades after the dip, I could easily explain why my grades were poor and, more importantly, I could use it as part of my defensive strategy to convince the highly competitive graduate school (Northwestern) that they could not reject me due to my bad grades. My story, although fairly generic, was simple and true: When I got to college, I didn't understand how to study. The social life distracted me and my parents stopped paying my way (the dip). Once I started paying my own way, I got more serious and began to apply myself. I was more selective about my activities and I was able to turn around academically. Voila! It's the classic "late-bloomer" story and it works!

To implement your defensive strategy, you must have a way to communicate your grade story to the admissions counselor (they will already have your grades, so don't send an actual chart). To do this you have a couple of options. First, you can reference your GPA and tell your story in your application cover letter.[40] Keep it brief and to the point. You want to plant the seed of hope, not create a big sob story about your dead grandmother or how teachers were out to get you. You can also make sure your references are aware of your grades so they can tell your grade story for you when they contact the college. This is an excellent conversation for your reference and the admissions counselor to have. Remember, your grade story is a defensive move. Do not make it your main story. It will *not* work on its own. You still need to implement a complete offensive strategy in order to succeed. It is for this reason that you should never write an essay about a grade story. Focus your essay on your NTA.

My defensive plan worked well. I was accepted to Northwestern,

---

40. Always, always include a cover letter every time you send something to the college.

where I continued to make good grades (making sure I had a good grade curve). Several years later, once my grades were on par with the caliber of student the college wanted, I was ready to apply to University of Chicago.

By the way, many people will imply that if you have poor grades you are doomed to unemployment and poverty. This is not true. Hardly anybody ever asks about your GPA outside the education world. A degree is a degree no matter what your grades were. When you apply for a job, it is far more important to be able to show that you were able to listen to instructions, start a project, and finish it. That's pretty much what college is all about.

Types of Grade Stories

It is possible to blow it by telling the wrong type of grade story. My story, the late-bloomer story, is the most basic and usually the safest bet. The late-bloomer story simply tells the college that you are now mature and responsible enough to get good grades. You may *think* that you already were mature and responsible, but it doesn't matter. What matters is that the college feels comfortable that you are now a person who can handle the work.

Hardship stories are also popular, but you need to be careful how you discuss your hardship, because the story can backfire. A hardship story describes an unforeseen event in your life that made it difficult for you to concentrate on school and thus, your grades suffered. Illness is a classic hardship. Some kids come down with a serious illness, like cancer, that hurts their grades. In these cases, a college will respect your perseverance. Not only is an illness like this a legitimate hardship story, but your experience will likely be an NTA as well. Lesser illnesses, like mono, can also be used, but a college won't buy it if the impact lasted too long. Getting a cold or breaking your leg are pretty weak stories that sound more like grade excuses than grade stories. Depression or mental illness is generally a no-no. Colleges don't want to deal with your history of instability even if you have it under control. Try and go with the late-bloomer story if your illness or hardship isn't major. If you're not sure if it's major, then it probably isn't. Ask around. I recently read a hardship story from a kid who said that his hardship was the summer he and his family had to drive through the desert with the heater on so the engine wouldn't overheat. Bad story!

Work stories can be tricky. Sometimes kids use work as a hardship. Working is *not* a hardship under any circumstances. If you think working is a hardship, you have a tough life ahead of you! Working, however, can be a grade story if your work was due to someone else's hardship. A parent, for example, may become disabled or unemployed. In this case you go to work in response to another person's hardship. In fact, you *happily* went to work to pick up the slack. If your father was injured on the job and disability payments weren't enough to cover the rent, so you stepped up to the plate and did your part, then you will earn the respect of the admissions counselor. If you tell the same story but pitch it as "poor me," you will fail. Always tell your story from an angle of personal growth.

If you have a physical disability, feel free to discuss it during the admissions process. Colleges always like to reach out to students with physical disabilities because it plays well to their tendency toward diversity. Students with physical disabilities are assets to the learning environment because they bring a different perspective. Physical disabilities can also be an NTA.

Learning disabilities can also be a grade story. If you have a diagnosed learning disability, you may be able to use it to your advantage during the admissions process. Colleges are happy to accommodate learning disabled students as long as they show they can overcome their disability and learn the material. To get the story right, make sure you describe the circumstances under which you discovered or were diagnosed with the disability and the specific steps taken to resolve or mitigate the impact on your GPA. Next, show how your GPA improved after you took the new steps. It's okay if you took a semester or so to turn things around. As long as the trend is up, then you are in good shape. If you have more than one dip, you are in trouble. Colleges don't want to see someone with an understanding of their own learning disability slip back into unproductive patterns. Learning disabilities are there to be overcome. It's not easy, but you need to show a college that you can do it.

The same goes for Attention Deficit Disorder (ADD). If you are diagnosed with ADD and are prescribed medication, show the positive impact the medication had on your GPA. Prior to medication, your inability to concentrate should have had a notable impact on your GPA; after medication, you should be able to demonstrate yourself as a significantly better student.

Whenever possible, however, go with the late-bloomer story. It is safer and quicker than other kinds of grade stories. Late-bloomer stories show that you are a different person who has gotten their academic act together. All other stories assume that a good student has had things in the way that prevented success. *Only* use a hardship or work story if your grade curve has multiple dips.

Hardship and work stories require you to get into details with the admissions counselor who then must make a judgment call with regard to your sincerity and the relative impact on your GPA. They would prefer not to be put in that position. My father came down with a debilitating disease while I was in high school. The disease was serious, and he became permanently disabled. After my sophomore year, I paid the lion's share of my own expenses in college. While I could have turned this into a work story and told of how I happily worked my way through college, I played it safe and went with the late-bloomer story. My job turned out to be my NTA, and I got a lot more mileage from it.

The problem with any grade story is that you have to eventually make good grades. And, if you need a grade story in the first place, you probably haven't figured out how to make good grades in the past. This is the exact problem that I faced. However, as I said before, I eventually figured it out and, to my surprise, it was actually *less* work than making bad grades.

Getting Good Grades

When I was in college, I encountered a series of events that forever changed my academic life. The first was a chemistry class I took during my sophomore year. The class was divided into two parts, the lecture and the lab. The lecture met twice per week for an hour and a half. During the lecture part of the class, you listened to a professor drone on about chemistry. You were supposed to take notes. The lectures roughly corresponded to the experiments during the lab part of the class. Labs met once a week for five hours. The class grade was a combination of the lab grade and the lecture grade. The lecture grade was based on a series of written exams and the lab grade was based on lab reports and the accuracy of the results.

I received a D in the class.

I went to speak with the professor to try and negotiate a better grade. He said he had already been generous with the D. Here is where the weird part comes in: the reason the professor had been generous and gave me a passing grade was because I had one of the *highest lab grades* in the course. I was awesome at the lab. I was so good, in fact, that the other students came to *me* for help. It was a five-hour class, but I was always done in less than three. The professor said I was a "brilliant" chemist. I was baffled. How could I be such a natural hotshot in the lab but such a miserable failure in the lecture? What was I missing? It wasn't as if I never studied; I did study. Did I need to study (gasp) harder?

The next event came the next semester. I went out on a few dates with the least intelligent girl I had ever met. She was quite nice and very attractive, but I was shocked at how difficult it was to carry on a meaningful conversation with her. It was almost as if she was putting on an act just for me![41] What was really strange about this girl was the fact that she was on a *full academic scholarship* to college. She had straight A's! In fact, she had never received a B in all her life! Her classes weren't lame classes either. She wanted to be a physical therapist and she was taking hard classes—she even got an A in chemistry! Who was this person and how did she do it? Was she just smarter than me?

I pondered these things as I started working harder to pull

---

41. She wasn't. Several of my friends dated her too, with the same complaint.

myself out of the dip. I tried to find classes that interested me, so I started taking some marketing classes. My grades weren't good enough to get into the advertising program, so I had to pick another major. I chose communications. I worked hard, studied hard, and began to pull my grades up. I knew that I wanted to go to a highly competitive graduate school and that my grades had to be better.

Panic ensued. My grades began to plateau. I was slipping back! I knew I had to forge ahead, but I began to slip into old habits. Then one day I got a break—a break that changed everything. I was taking a Rhetoric class and I was getting a C average. There was an optional term paper that could increase your grade by one full letter, but only if you had a B or better on the midterm exam. The paper was due a week after the midterm, but I didn't bother doing it because I was resolved to get a C in the class. The day before the term paper was due our midterm exams were returned. I got a B+ on the midterm. I was floored. What luck! This was my chance.

If I could somehow complete a fifteen-page term paper by the following afternoon, I had a chance at receiving a decent grade in the class. But how? I immediately got a copy of the assignment and headed over to the library. As part of the assignment I had to cite and reference at least five resources. I looked up about ten books. Next I sat down and outlined the assignment so I would know what quotes I needed to get from the books. Each question had a point value ranging from one to five. I figured I needed at least one idea for each point, so I made sure my outline had enough information. I found the quotes, finished my outline, and headed home—I was on a roll. That night I went out to see my friend's band play. It rocked!

The next morning I got out my notes and began typing. The outline made the work go much faster than usual. I was writing as fast as I could. I only stopped to cross-reference my notes with the point values on the assignment sheet. Within a couple of hours I had a fifteen-page paper ready to turn in.[42] I went to class and turned in the paper. I got a 98 percent and finished the class with a B. The next semester I got straight A's.

These three experiences led me to my understanding of good grades. The first realization I made was that getting good grades doesn't mean you are smart and being smart doesn't mean you will get good grades. Growing up, people were always telling me that I was smart, so I guess I spent a lot of time just waiting to get good grades. That's the lesson I learned from the girl I dated who I thought could barely outsmart a brick.

The next lesson was from the chemistry class. I loved the labs and really understood the material. However, in order to get good grades, you need to understand that our education is delivered within a very specific structure. You need to apply that structure to learning so you can later recall it in the same structure. In the chemistry class, the lab was the understanding part and the lecture was the structure. I didn't connect the dots until I was forced to.

Getting good grades is often about learning some basic material and then answering a few questions about it. When I wrote the Rhetoric term paper, I didn't have time to mess around. I had to concentrate very hard on what the professor wanted. I dissected every question and outlined every answer. For the first time in my life, I actually answered the questions. My chemistry class

---

42. It took a little tweaking of the font size and margins to get to fifteen pages.

taught me that I had learned the material—I had always learned the material. What I wasn't doing was answering the questions the professor was asking. Sound simple? It is. If you are making bad grades, it may be because you either aren't learning the material, or perhaps, you aren't answering the right questions. This is why some people study very, very hard and still get bad grades—they aren't answering the right questions.

Every teacher and professor develops their own style of teaching and has their own expectations of their students. When they create and administer tests, they have very specific preconceptions with regard to how their questions will be answered. In other words, they have the answers in their mind when they create the test. It is your job to understand the question well enough to be able to tell what they want. If you are going to class as expected, you should get to know the teacher's personality. If you are unsure, ask them. Ask them to go over past tests with you. Ask them to explain their reasoning. Tell them you want to better understand their expectations and how they created the test. All this information will help you answer the question correctly.

Once I figured out how to make good grades, I began to love school. I learned just as much, but I worked much, much less.

CARROT:

For a more detailed explanation of what it means to correctly answer the question, visit CollegePeas.com and enter the word ANSWER in the CARROT Box.

Your Turn

My grade problem boiled down to my inability to answer the questions that were being asked. I was learning and understanding, but I just didn't pay close enough attention to the questions. Your problem may be different, but it's probably not much different. Before you start studying harder, make sure you carefully read the question. Rewrite the question in bullet form and make sure you have an answer for each part of the question. Do this even for quantitative classes.

One of my roommates was a philosophy major. He learned an incredible amount and went on to become a top-performing salesperson making hundreds of thousands of dollars per year. Now he designs and builds houses. He, too, had terrible grades. His problem was the same as mine. He was learning the material but failing to answer the questions.

The other potential problem is that you know how to answer the questions but don't actually know the answer. This is a different problem, and if you have it, you may not really be trying in the first place. If you are actually *trying* to make good grades, you tend to study, read the books, go to class,[43] and engage one-on-one with your professors. People who aren't trying to get good grades can be found doing just about any other activity, such as watching TV, sleeping, or playing Frisbee.[44]

This is a different problem that can also be overcome. You'll have to figure it out on your own because I personally don't know what to tell you. I'm pretty confident you fall into the

---

43. Sit in the front row. Good students generally sit in the front of the class; bad students generally sit in the back.

44. Frisbee is a super-fun thing to do in college.

first category, though. Most people I know seemed to learn a lot in college.

Remember this important lesson: smart people don't necessarily make good grades and people who make good grades aren't necessarily smart. In reality, being smart does not guarantee good grades. Everyone thinks it does, but it doesn't. If you weren't blessed with book smarts, that's too bad, but don't let that stand in the way of your success. If you have gotten this far in your education, I'm certain that the effort required to make good grades is *well* within your grasp.

Negotiating Good Grades

There is another way to improve your grades: negotiating (aka smooth-talking). Negotiating better grades is a completely legitimate way to raise your GPA. One thing to remember about negotiating better grades is that it's not about getting a break. You have to show the professor that you actually deserve a better grade. Many people think it's easier to simply go lay a sob story on the professor, shed a few tears, and if necessary, fake a seizure. This may work and it may work well, but it will never actually help you become a better student.

When negotiating better grades, give your professor an offer they can't refuse. First, make sure you have done all the homework and all the extra credit work. Next, don't skip class. If you can show that you came to every class and did all the work, then the professor has nobody to blame but themselves!

During my final semester in college, I was set to get a 4.0. I had an A going in one of my classes, so I skipped the extra credit assignment. I got a B on the final and thus, earned a B in the class. I went to negotiate a better grade, but I was denied. I asked the professor if I could do the extra credit assignment. He said no, the assignment was past due, and he had already submitted his final grades. I went home, did the extra credit assignment anyway, and stuck it under his door with copies of all my homework assignments. I wrote him a letter explaining how I had been a poor student, but I was working hard to pull up my grades, blah, blah, blah. It worked. I didn't get a freebie; I got a bump because I showed that I was willing to do what it takes.

It doesn't always work. But give it a try; you'll be surprised on how often it does work.

Standardized Tests Are a Game

There are two elephants marching around any college admissions conversation. The first is the GPA elephant and the second is the dreaded standardized test elephant. The former gives you plenty of chances to tame it; the second is a one- (or two- or three-) shot deal that can tarnish an otherwise solid application. So, at this point it is important to say a few words about test scores. They are purposely downplayed in this book because they mean less and less next to a good NTA, a broken Zone, a direct shot at the Nerve, and a good grade story. Test scores are good when a college doesn't have much else to go on. In fact, I was at a recent admissions conference where the keynote speaker was the admissions dean from a very competitive college that was test-optional.[45] The guy said point-blank that all things being equal, they're going to accept the student who submits the test scores over the student

---

45. Lots of colleges are going test-optional these days.

who does not—even though they are test-optional. It sounds weird, but it's true. Note, however, that he said "all things being equal." You don't have to worry—you are going to stand out big time and your test scores will mean less. Don't get me wrong, test scores are important. This book is about what to do if your grades and test scores aren't great.

The most important thing to keep in mind about standardized tests is this: they are a game. That's right—a game. All of the content covered on a standardized test (SAT or ACT) is material you have already covered by the time you are a junior in high school—all of it. The tests introduce nothing new. In fact, the material really isn't that complicated. What makes the test seem so hard is 1) you think it's going to ask you for information you don't already know and 2) you don't know the rules of the game. Now that you know the material is all regurgitated high school mumbo-jumbo, you can concentrate on the rules of the game.

There is only a handful of question "types" asked on the tests and most of them are pretty straightforward. To learn the rules, you'll need to read a few books about the tests, or better yet, take a test prep course. The test prep companies are all about teaching you the rules and the tricks to getting a better score—their existence depends on it.

If you don't bother to learn the rules, then taking practice tests is a pretty big waste of time. You should still take a few, but if you learn the rules first, you will get much more out of the time you spend. If you take practice tests without learning the rules, you won't learn much because the test you take will be different than the practice test. Practice tests are for practicing the rules of the game—not for learning information. After you learn the rules of the game, take lots of practice tests. Practice, practice, practice! As you practice, you need to first figure out what type of question is being asked and then apply the rules to finding the best answer.

Here is another way you can tell it's a game: you are better off *guessing*[46] than leaving an answer blank on the SAT. Standardized tests are *not* scored the way most of your other tests are. Your test prep course will tell you the rules of scoring too so you can use them to your advantage.

If you can't afford a test prep course, try asking the test prep company if they offer scholarships or discounts to students who can't afford a test prep course. If that doesn't work, why not try to talk local businesses into sponsoring your test? Maybe you can start an organization that organizes test prep scholarships for needy kids—a great NTA!

There are online test prep courses that are much less expensive than the classroom-based courses. I have a friend who started a website called PrepMe.com—he claims they have better success than the classroom-based courses and they cost considerably less. If that doesn't work, there are some free test prep classes online. They are teaching the same basic rules but some teach the rules better than others.

If all else fails, then you can go to the library and read some test prep books. They usually have the same content as the classes except there is nobody on-hand to spoon-feed you the material and hold your hand through the tricky parts.

One last thing—get a good night's sleep before your test and don't worry about it once you leave the testing facility. No matter what your score is, forget about it. If you think you can improve it,

---

46. Test prep classes actually teach you how to guess for best results.

you can always try again later; if you don't think you can improve it, then move on. There are more important things at stake.

I know a woman who got accepted to a competitive under-graduate college in spite of the fact that she was in the bottom 9 percent[47] on her SAT. She had a good NTA and good grades. Her test scores didn't matter. She later continued on to a very competitive graduate school after scoring a 400 on her GMAT,[48] which is about as low as you can go. I promise: if colleges want you, they will look beyond your shortcomings.

Community Colleges

One of the best ways to land yourself into a competitive school is to not apply in the first place. If you are a 100-percent out person, you can make a legitimate move by sitting this round out and taking a less competitive route to community college for a few years to create your defensive plan. Most colleges, even some of the most competitive colleges, accept transfer students start-ing sophomore or junior year. This is because so many freshmen and sophomores wind up dropping out or transferring out. In a typical college, there are fewer juniors and seniors than there are freshmen and sophomores. A couple of years in a community college could be just what you need to build your defensive plan and get a grade story. (When you are finally ready to apply, keep in mind that all the previous rules still apply. Your chances still go up if you have an NTA, break the Zone, and hit the Nerve.)

The community college route offers a number of real, tangible benefits. First, it will allow you get some of the basic classes out of the way and apply with less competition—fewer people apply

---

47. Yep, most people could have slept through the test and done better!

48. GMAT is like the SAT for business schools.

as transfer students (there are also fewer spots, but the odds will likely work in your favor). By the time you apply to the school of your choice, you will become even more valuable to them because they will need to fill their upper classes.

Next, you can save a boatload of cash. Community colleges are a lot cheaper than competitive colleges. You can probably keep living with your parents and work on your NTA in your spare time. If your parents whine that you didn't get into a competitive college, you can remind them that you are biding your time and show them how much money you are saving.

Also, community colleges often have more opportunity for personalized attention. I know a man who really made community colleges work for him. Instead of going to college, he enrolled in community college. He concentrated on the tough classes and worked one-on-one with professors. He didn't finish his two-year degree because he transferred out to a very competitive four-year college. He didn't finish his degree there either because he transferred again. This time he went into medical school at the University of Michigan. He graduated from one of the most competitive medical schools in the country in less time and with less debt by going the community college route. He never earned his associate or his bachelor's degree; he skipped, skipped to medical school!

Another key benefit to community colleges is that after a few decent years, your high school grades become irrelevant! So, if you're anything like me, you can bury your past deep down inside your secret place in just a couple of semesters. Most colleges don't care about your high school grades if you can show them two to four college semesters of solid performance. This is your first, true get-out-of-jail-free card! Savor the flavor because chances like this are rare in life.

Many colleges have close ties to community colleges and routinely accept transfers from them. If you are serious about attending the competitive college of your choice, find out where the nearby community college is and sign up. You can live right next to the competitive college of your dreams and mingle with the lucky students who were actually accepted. You can also get to know the admissions department and let them know you are working hard to get admitted.[49]

Don't underestimate the value of community colleges. They can be used to give you a real leg up on the competition. Most of them do not have competitive admission and their credits usually transfer. However, save your books and class notes just in case— you may need them to negotiate credit hours when you get into your four-year competitive college.[50]

Graduate Schools

Even if you never get into a competitive undergraduate school, the good news is that there is one last option to get a degree from a competitive school. It's called graduate school. Graduate school is where you go to earn a master's degree, doctoral degree (PhD), or professional degree (like medicine or law). These programs usually require an undergraduate degree, although it's not out

---

49. If you ever saw the movie *Rudy*, you know that he went to a local community college before getting into Notre Dame.

50. My sister transferred her junior year, and her new college would not accept her transfer credits. She had saved *all* her textbooks, notes, and tests. She used them to negotiate the transfer of all her class credits because the classes covered the same material. If you are going to transfer, save your class materials.

of the question for them to waive the degree requirement if you meet certain academic requirements.

I personally took advantage of the graduate school route. However, I used exactly the same principles for getting into graduate school that I used to get into college. I started preparing for graduate school about a year or two before I graduated from college (I was on a five-year plan). I set my sights high. I had been accepted to several competitive undergraduate institutions in spite of my terrible academic record. I knew that I wanted to immediately continue on to graduate school[51] and be accepted at graduate schools that were *highly* competitive. I chose two highly competitive schools—Northwestern and Washington University in St. Louis. My offensive plan included a good NTA (I started several businesses in college and I was active in student government), I broke the Zone (only two kids from Kansas applied to Northwestern), I leveraged my team, and I forged a new path by seeking out a local alumnus for the interview instead of traveling to campus. My defensive plan was my nice grade curve and my grade story. Even though my final GPA was more than a full point below Northwestern's average, I was still accepted.

Several years later I returned again to graduate school at another highly competitive college, the University of Chicago. Although I had a much more solid academic foundation by that time, I still used the ideas in this book to ensure that I had a place in the program.

---

51. Many competitive and highly competitive graduate programs, especially business schools, like you to have a few years of work experience under your belt before you apply. You will get more out of your education if you have experience, but if you can go right away, do it. You will start reaping the financial benefits earlier in life.

Chapter 9

A FEW FINAL THOUGHTS

Good, qualified students get rejected from competitive colleges every day. It causes much angst and controversy when a solid straight-A student who was captain of the swim team, member of the yearbook staff, and volunteered for Habitat for Humanity gets passed over in favor of some other kid who got worse grades and didn't participate in any regular extracurricular activities. The applicant and those around her are outraged at this seemingly blatant oversight on the part of the admissions department. What isn't always clear is that often the kid who got in was so engaged in his NTA that he didn't have time for sports and clubs. He was busy with his website on which he posted the pictures he took and descriptions he wrote of every bird in his state. To most people it seemed like a silly hobby. To the college it was a wonderful NTA.

The next time that happens, ask yourself, did this person have an NTA? Did she break the Zone? Did she try a backdoor approach?

Did she leverage her team? Did she stuff the ballot box? Even the most hardworking students overlook these simple concepts every day. Grades aren't everything, school activities aren't everything, and perfectly written essays aren't everything. They are certainly *something*, but definitely not everything. When the exceptional student gets passed over for admissions, it's because the college already had plenty of kids like them and they wanted to try something new. They wanted to take some chances. Taking chances is the only way to move ahead. Contrary to popular belief, college admissions departments don't make a lot of mistakes. When was the last time you saw a competitive college go out of business or even drop off the competitive college list? They know the business quite well.

Colleges want students who will 1) complete their degrees and 2) become active alumni.[52] Their safest bets are the kids who get good grades and good test scores. It is fairly clear that these people are engaged in their education and have an affinity for the work. But the top students aren't necessarily the best students; they are merely the safest bets. When they see your willingness to go where no teen has gone before, they will get excited and their willingness to give you a chance goes up.

The ideas in this book aren't designed to help you get away with anything. You're not fooling anyone. Admissions counselors weren't born yesterday. This book is about being the kind of student that admissions counselors actually want. It's about being an interested and interesting student. And, ultimately, it's about becoming a better student.

In the end, I became a successful student at highly competitive colleges. I didn't con my way in with tricks; I presented myself

---

52. An active alumnus is one who either donates money or time because they love their alma mater.

honestly, and I stood out because I did the things outlined in this book. For me it was luck; for you it will be action.

I think the colleges who admitted me made the right choice even though I was an academic risk. As a college student, I was very involved in student activities and student government as an undergraduate. I am now an active alumnus of the graduate programs I attended. I've been a guest speaker for classes at both Northwestern and University of Chicago. I've hired interns from them and I've even donated money in spite of the fact that I borrowed more money than it takes to choke a donkey. I even represented KU at a recent college fair in my area. For these colleges, taking a chance on me paid off.

Rejecting Your Acceptance

When your big, fat letter of acceptance comes in the mail from your competitive college, you will have done what you set out to do. You can be proud of your accomplishment. Cherish the moment, read every word, call your grandparents, show your friends, and make sure your guidance counselor and references know that you appreciate the part they played.

But now that you have your acceptance letter, don't be afraid to say *no*! Just because you were accepted to a competitive college does not mean you have to actually attend the college. One of the first things in this book was the idea that fit is the most important issue with regard to college. Make sure that you choose the right college for you regardless of the name or how competitive it is. People turn down competitive colleges all the time without losing any of the joy or admiration that comes with getting accepted in the first place.

I recently spoke to an intern who has a friend who turned down a coveted Ivy League college so she could attend her state college. My hat's off to the girl for getting into the Ivies, but the true evidence of her intelligence was her decision to choose the college that was a better fit. She chose the state college because it was closer to home, it offered the business program she wanted, and they aggressively recruited her—they even offered her a very nice scholarship. It's nice to be wanted, and the state college knows that anything they can do to welcome students who might otherwise go to an Ivy League college will raise their own educational status.

Don't get me wrong, Ivy League colleges are awesome and lots of students and alumni love them, but there are colleges out there that are aggressively trying to find the right students even though they are competitive colleges. I know one southern college that really wants top students. They will provide a full scholarship to any National Merit Finalist. This includes eight semesters of tuition, room and board, $1,000 annual living stipend, $2,000 research grant, and a laptop computer! I personally said no to all the competitive colleges on my list and chose, instead, to attend a non-competitive state school. I never looked back.

All colleges have a lot to offer. They can help you build a good life for yourself and your family. Going to a competitive college doesn't guarantee success, but going to a competitive college does force you to set a standard of excellence in your own life. This book is about developing a plan to achieve your goals.

Going to a competitive college is about you doing your best

in spite of your past failures. Anyone can succeed if they have a genuine interest. I hope this book can help show you the way!

Unintended Consequences

Following the advice in this book will cause another unintended consequence besides landing you an admissions letter to a competitive college. Following the advice in this book will help you grow up a little.

Choosing an NTA will help you venture out on your own and be your own person. My NTAs were raising homing pigeons and starting businesses. I was forced to figure things out on my own. My parents weren't that into pigeons[53] and they weren't terribly business savvy. They had to back off and let me do things on my own because they didn't know how to help.

Stepping out of my Zone meant that I was willing to cut the umbilical cord and take care of myself. Being so far away from home meant that I couldn't swing by home to do my laundry or get a home-cooked meal. Lots of my friends in college had these things, and I sometimes wished I had them too, but not having them meant I had to learn how to take care of myself.

By taking charge of my application team, I learned how to manage projects and people. The people I managed were older and wiser than me, yet they all happily worked to forward my own personal agenda. This is a skill, by the way, that will serve you well throughout your life.

The unintended consequence of my actions was that I eventually learned to love learning and I eventually learned to be a good student. Looking back I'm confident that I made the right moves.

---

53. Understatement of the year.

Not all the right moves, but enough of the right moves that I don't look back with regret.

Up, Up, and Away!

College is a good time, a great time, a fantastic time. Everything goes. Everyone wants to learn new things and everyone who gets through comes out on the other side better prepared for life than they were when they started. In the next four to six years, you will have done all sorts of things you never thought possible.

While getting into college isn't the most stressful part, it sure comes close for a lot of students, but it doesn't have to be. Getting into college seems to be the culmination of four hard years in high school. It seems to be the only thing that stands between you and all your dreams. That's too bad. Getting into college does not have to be an unfortunate series of events that throws your life into chaos. It is within your reach. You can do it. Simply follow the advice in this book, collect your acceptance letters, make your choice based on fit, and never look back.

INDEX

ACKNOWLEDGMENTS

This is my first book. I've always wanted to write a book, but I never expected it to be about getting into college. If this book helps you get into college then you and I have a few people we should thank, because without them it never would have happened.

First, I want to extend a general thank you to the many people who read drafts of the book and provided feedback and encouragement. This includes coworkers, advisors, students, and parents. Nothing beats good old-fashioned constructive criticism and the book is far better because of it.

Julie and Chuck Bukrey (my in-laws) as well as Suzanne Moyer, Robin Chung, and Kendra Foley (my mom and sisters) all gave me the encouragement I needed to push through to the end. My wife, Anne, read many drafts and then fed my ego by telling me I was smart and talented, a critical part of the process that could not have been done better by anyone else. And my young children, Anson and Merrily, in addition to constant interruption and distraction, provided inspiration to write a message that I hope will be relevant and important when they start their own college search. I hope they are as proud of me as I am of them.

I couldn't have been luckier to find Sourcebooks. A special thanks to Dominique Raccah and Peter Lynch for seeing the potential in this project and to those who worked on it including Steve O'Rear, Sarah Cardillo, and Dojna Shearer. I look forward to working with the rest of the Sourcebooks team.

A special thanks to my attorney, Sallie Randolph, who gave me a crash course in publishing contracts. I think she got more than she bargained for with me, and I really appreciate her work.

Lastly, thank you, the reader, for reading the book and for not skipping the Acknowledgments page.

Most sincerely,

Mike Moyer

ABOUT THE AUTHOR

Mike Moyer had a 2.04 GPA from high school, yet he figured out how to beat the odds and get accepted to competitive colleges. He is the cofounder of Cappex.com and the founder of College Peas, a company dedicated to helping kids beat the admissions odds. Mike has a BA in communication from the University of Kansas, an MS in integrated marketing communication from Northwestern University, and an MBA from the University of Chicago. He lives in the Chicago area with his wife and two children. Visit CollegePeas.com to read Mike's blog.

CollegePeas™

(www.CollegePeas.com)

What you do in high school determines where you will go to college. Getting ready for college includes a healthy dose of P's, including: PrePare, Plan, aPPly, and Pick, as well as others. The earlier you get started, the better your chances of getting into the college of your dreams. Learn more about getting ready for college and how you can get an edge over the competition. Visit CollegePeas.com for your serving of College Peas and Carrots!